Lost Inns of the Yorks'

TIME, PLEASE!

'Lost' Inns, Pubs and Alehouses of the Yorkshire Dales

David S. Johnson

NORTH CRAVEN HERITAGE TRUST

NORTH
CRAVEN

HERITAGE

www.northcravenheritage.org.uk
http://storiesinstone.org.uk

ISBN 978-1-9160727-6-3
British Library Cataloguing in Publication data
A catalogue record for this book is available from the British Library
Design and Layout: D&AW www.dandaw.com
Proudly Printed by:

Front cover:
The Naked Man, Settle in 2019 (John Asher)

Production of this book was part-funded by Stories in Stone, a scheme of conservation and community projects concentrated in the Ingleborough area. The scheme was developed by the Ingleborough Dales Landscape Partnership, led by Yorkshire Dales Millennium Trust and supported by the National Heritage Lottery Fund.

Acknowledgements

I extend my gratitude to Alison Armstrong, John Asher, Pat Carroll, Sheila Gordon, Paul Hypher, Margaret and John Owen, Ken Pearce, Mike Slater, Will Swales and Sue Wrathmell – they will know why. I also thank John Frankland of North Yorkshire Library Service (Skipton) for facilitating reproduction of images from the Rowley Collection; Mary Painter of Blackburn Central Library for consent to reproduce images from the Shaw Collection; and Julia Skinner for images from The Francis Frith Collection. Thanks are also due to the committee of the North Craven Heritage Trust for funding and logistical support, and for believing in this project; and to the Stories in Stone team for funding and support.

Author's Note

The aim of this book is to present a series of snapshots of drinking establishments in the Yorkshire Dales through the ages. No attempt has been made to be comprehensive: given the space available, that would be impossible. Rather, what is presented here is a representative sample of former alehouses, inns and pubs. The author has lived in Upper Ribblesdale since 1983 so there is bound to be a geographical bias towards Craven. Areas which might appear under-represented are asked for forgiveness – no snub is intended. Every effort has been made to contact copyright holders of historical images in this book. If you believe you have been overlooked, please contact the publisher. If anyone whose name should have been mentioned has been omitted, apologies are offered: due acknowledgement will be made in any reprint of the book.

Several people have suggested to the author – hopefully with tongue in cheek – that it might be more interesting to write about pubs that are not 'lost'! If justification were deemed necessary, it is that a study of former inns and pubs has much to say about social aspects of life in the past. Inns addressed the needs of travellers on foot, horseback or in wheeled vehicles: given that a day's journey then can be achieved now in fifteen minutes, the proliferation of former inns will come as no surprise. The hierarchy of 'inns' – bait-houses, hedge alehouses, minor inns and posting and coaching inns – also speaks of the social hierarchy that prevailed in the past. The incredible number of pubs – the 'local' – in towns and villages has much to say about how people socialised in the past, how men's social life differed from that of their wives. Looking back with a twenty-first-century perspective on past social and gender mores will unsettle many people today but we cannot change the past. Nor can we change the stark reality that life for working men – in lead mines, quarries, on the road for weeks on end as a drover or packhorse man, in textile mills – was a long hard grind, and pubs were seen as an escape. We have no right to judge them by our standards.

Grid references are provided for premises outside settlements. Distribution maps have not been provided, except for central Skipton and Settle: half the fun of seeking out 'lost' inns' and pubs is the process itself. All modern photographs were taken by the author. As many pub names omit the apostrophe, the same convention has been adopted throughout the book.

A gazetteer of former licensed premises in the Dales is available online at http://www.northcravenheritage.org.uk/EVENTS/F/NCHT/LostInns.htm

Contents

Introduction

It is not just birds, bees and butterflies that have seen a dramatic fall in numbers in recent decades: there has been an equally catastrophic decline in the number of pubs across the country, in rural areas as well as urban. A current campaign – Long Live the Local – points out that '3 pubs a day close their doors for good'. That equates to nearly 1100 over one year which must be a frightening statistic for pub aficionados but it compares favourably with recent years, with 2009 plumbing the depths seeing 2704 close whereas 2012 saw only 832 calling time for ever, though by 2015 the total had crept up again to 1404. Looked at through another prism, in 1900 England and Wales had 102,000 licensed premises of one kind or another; by 1960 the total had plummeted to 69,000, but rose to 110,000 by the end of the millennium. This last statistic comes with a health warning, however: in 1900 the vast majority would have been hostelries; in our time not so. Think of your nearest town – how many pubs are still operational? Think also where else you can purchase alcohol – supermarkets, shops, wine and bottle bars, cafés and restaurants. The decline in numbers reflects how much alcohol we now consume and, tellingly, where and how we consume it.

There is a plethora of names – labels – that were attached to hostelries over the centuries. The word 'hostelry' now has pejorative undertones, but this is unfair because until relatively recent times it was synonymous with 'inn' – and what's wrong with that? It derives from the French, and ultimately from the Latin *hospitalis* or *hospitium* (hospitable, or lodging/inn). Back then, a hospital but had a much broader range of functions and was not just a place to go when you were ill. Through the monastic era abbeys established such facilities either on their far-flung estates or on routeways in-between. They were called 'spitals' and offered succour and basic accommodation to the traveller and, if necessary, attention to their ailments. St Nicholas, on the byroad from Richmond to Easby Abbey, was founded as the Hospital of St Nicholas by the earl of Richmond in the reign of Henry II (r. 1154-89) specifically to care for the needy and to provide lodging for pilgrims and travellers in need – a true spital. [1] Out of the spital concept arose the ever-present alehouse, found in every village, on every road, and in every town. Simply put, an alehouse was any private house that sold ale or, later, beer; the thirsty traveller would have recognised an alehouse open for business from the pole, or stake, hung or standing outside the house, often with some kind of foliage attached. This was the precursor to the pub or inn sign. In towns they normally just sold alcohol but in remote areas often offered basic food and communal accommodation, even if only above the stable, outhouse or barn. This is where the modern (slang) word 'doss' originates – a doss was the right to bed down in the straw or whatever. The most basic and remote alehouses had the label 'hedge alehouse' suggesting little more comfort was to be had than out in the open air; or 'bait-house', bait meaning food but again implying bargain-basement accommodation.

A variation on the alehouse theme was the 'bough house' which was also a temporary feature found in villages or market towns when livestock or produce fairs were in operation. Again, any householder could set themselves up in this way merely by brewing some ale and putting a bough – often of holly – outside the front door to let visitors know ale – and a good time – was to be had there.

More permanent establishments sold ale or beer throughout the year so they became known by the keeper's name or by their reputation as a brewer: these were 'beer-houses'. Some keepers either lacked the facilities or the knowledge to brew the ale or beer so they bought in supplies from those who did, thus, rather than being called a beer-house, these were 'tippling houses'.

In larger towns 'taverns' were a common feature: originally, a tavern only or mostly sold wine (and maybe spirits) rather than ale or beer, and many of them gained a certain reputation owing in no small part to Shakespeare's graphic tavern scenes. You went to a tavern to have a really good time. The writer and poet John Earle compared, in 1811, an alehouse with a tavern: the latter was 'where men are drunk with more credit and apology' than in the former. [2] One can perhaps detect a hint of snobbery here.

Genuine taverns are a rarity in the Dales: Richmond has its still-functional *Castle Tavern,* Skipton had *The Ship Tavern* at the bottom of Sheep Street, and Dent had *The Bridge Inn Tavern*, but were they ever true taverns? It is perhaps worth noting that the modern Welsh word for a pub or inn is *tafarn.*

The site of the former Ship Tavern on Ship Corner, Skipton

Every large town, market town and major routeway had its complement of inns; settlements on long-distance coaching routes served by inns came to be referred to as 'thoroughfare towns'. The term 'inn' first began to appear in the fifteenth century and they all offered the same set of facilities – several ground-floor rooms for eating ('victuals') and drinking, and set meals called 'ordinaries' which were sold at a fixed price (today's set menu) – and sleeping accommodation upstairs. Over time, and as railways replaced long-distance coaches, many inns lost their wherewithal and status either to close or to reinvent themselves as a public house or even a lowly beer-house.

Feb. 20 1822

THE KINGS HEAD

J.LIGHTFOOT, MASHAM.

	L	S	D
Eating 10 Dinners	1		
Wine & Negus	2	14	6
Punch			
Tea & Coffee			
Rum Brandy &c.		3	
Ale & Porter		2	6
Servants			
Hay & Corn			
Post Chaise			
Tobacco			
Washing			
Paper			

£4 : 0 : 0

An 'Ordinary' bill for a meal at the King's Head, Masham, 1822
(Author's collection)

Accommodation varied according to the traveller's budget: maybe a private room, maybe a shared room; going even further down the cost scale maybe just a shared bed within which, according to a contemporary description of a typical inn, everyone slept naked (and shared the bed bugs); or perhaps just a doss. The would-be early-seventeenth-century poet, John Taylor, wrote a little ditty having stayed overnight in an inn, and it neatly sums up his feelings:

From nasty rooms, that never felt brooms,
From excrements and all bad scents,
From children's bawling and caterwauling,
From grunting of hogs and barking of dogs,
From biting of fleas, I found no ease.

Antiquarian and renowned botanist Thomas Pennant visited Settle in 1773 while journeying northwards to Alston. Though, in his opinion, Settle resembled a 'shabby French town' he did find succour at the 'neatest and most comfortable little inn' he had ever stayed at, made better by the 'civility and attention of the landlady'. He did not identify it.

In the early nineteenth century, inns which enjoyed prime positions on the road, or within a town, established links with carriers or wagon owners and became what were called 'posting-houses' offering either cartage by wagon or passage in a coach following fixed routes on a fixed timetable.

Finally, and most recently, there appeared the ubiquitous 'pub' which is just a contraction of the earlier term 'public house': the former term first appeared c. 1669 but only came into common usage around 1800, the latter around 1812. Pubs grew out of existing beer-houses, alehouses or lesser inns. The pub was the 'local', somewhere for men (yes, dominantly men) to escape the daily grind and to give themselves a breathing space before going home to face domestic reality. One of this writer's grandfathers, a rather militant shop steward, professed that Victorian industrialists sited a pub on every other street corner in those endless rows of terraced houses with the prime intention of providing the workers (mostly men again) with a warm place where they could mingle with their pals, use whatever language they chose, to get quietly (or noisily) inebriated ... with the ultimate aim of the factory owners ensuring the men (and more so their long-suffering wives) would forever be short of money so would have to keep working and, furthermore, would forget all their grievances in the haze of the cigarette smoke and the oblivion induced by the beer. A worrying statistic from 1935, which rather backs up grandfather's protestations, suggested that 6 per cent of national income in this country was spent on alcohol. [3] A nineteenth-century fictional character, John Ridd, also adds weight to the quantity of alcohol routinely consumed, though this time in very different rural surroundings. In trying to reassure his Italian host that the English did not drink to excess, he retorted 'Nay ... not all day long ... Only a pint at breakfast-time, and a pint and a half at eleven o'clock, and a quart or so at dinner. And then no more till the afternoon; and half a gallon at supper time.' [4] He was not jesting.

An anonymous and undated rhyme felt obliged to drag women into the same drunken mire as men:

> There was an old woman. And what do you think?
> She lived upon nothing but victuals and drink;
> Victuals and drink were the whole of her diet,
> And yet this old woman would NEVER be quiet.

Ale and beer are two more words whose meaning has changed over time. Both were brewed from the same basic ingredients, namely water plus malt (from barley) except that beer had the addition of hops (a member of the hemp family, botanically *Humulus lupulus*). It is said that hops were first introduced to Britain from the near continent in the fourteenth century yet marine excavation, in 1970, of a late-tenth-century boat at Graveney (Kent) found its cargo included 5 tons of hops probably brought from the Rhineland, so what the hops were destined for is a mystery. [5] According to Pliny, hops did no good yet later (English) writers extolled its virtues: improve appetite, promote sleep, reduce tension, improve digestion, relieve bowel disorders, are probably all quite acceptable to most drinkers, but perhaps less so clear nausea and relieve headaches. Whatever their perceived benefits, hops-free ale was slowly and largely replaced by beer between c. 1400 and 1700. For a final word on the qualities of hops, a Cumbrian recipe for treating 'failing sickness' (seizures or epilepsy) advised adding the dried and powdered intestines of three goslings to a draught of ale with hops [6] – surely a clear case of kill or cure.

What became such a major part of the British liquid diet was 'small beer', that is ale or beer brewed from recycled mash, thereby with a much reduced alcohol content and weaker taste. Think of a reused tea bag, perhaps. Considerable quantities of small beer were a natural by-product of brewing strong beer. It was the main drink of young, old and thirsty workers.

Chapter 1

Historical Overview

There is nothing even remotely new about people feeling the urge to consume alcohol, all too often, it has to be said, to excess. It has been a recurring theme for millennia and we can readily envisage Bronze Age or Iron Age folk in the Dales making use of whatever ingredients were at hand to conjure up a brew. We know the Romans had a penchant for ale (and wine) but the absence of large civilian settlements in the Roman-period Dales probably rules out there having been a network of *diversoria* (alehouses) or *taberna* (taverns). For the Anglo-Saxon period, however, we can be more certain, largely thanks to the enormous amount of work done in North Craven in recent years on a range of settlement sites that have all proved occupation between the retreat of the Romans and the arrival of the Normans. We now know that people lived here in the early medieval centuries, we know they had links with other parts of the country, and that the southern Dales had close ties with a major ecclesiastical estate based on Addingham and Otley, with the Aire-Wenning gap having been the obvious through-route. It goes without saying that Anglo- Saxon cross-country travellers hereabouts could have stopped over at an *ealu-hūs* or *bēor-hūs* (ale or beer house) or a *cumen-hūs* (an inn or tavern).

As early as the eighth century the Anglo-Saxon kingdom of Northumbria, which included the Dales, enacted laws to forbid priests from frequenting taverns and, in the late tenth century, a royal edict tried to restrict the number of alehouses. [7] Needless to say, they failed miserably but generated endless legislative attempts through the centuries to curb excessive drinking and eliminate corruption and disregard for existing laws and regulations.

The Assize of Bread and Ale from 1267, in the reign of Henry III, fixed the maximum price at which ale could be sold based on the price of the barley it was made from, and a follow-up decree in the reign of Edward I (in 1283) set the price of best ale at 1½d a gallon and weak ale at 1d (in old pence, 'd' being short for *denarius*). Ale and bread, both being staple commodities, were lumped together for legal purposes and every local court had the right to hold the Assize of Bread and Ale. [8] Manor court records are invariably full of instances where alehouse keepers were hauled up for breaking the Assize – often repeatedly. It was so common for official ale-tasters (or conners) to find when doing their inspections that ale was either sold at the wrong price or had been watered down too much. Much of Malhamdale, in North Craven, lay within the estates of Bolton Priory and, at an unknown but thirteenth-century date, James of Eshton in Malhamdale was summoned to answer to the King concerning various matters including his infringement of the Assize. [9] The court record states *ass cervisi fract [assisam cervisium fractum]* – he had broken the assize of ale.

Further Acts followed in frustrated and almost desperate attempts to stamp royal authority on alehouse keepers. The Assize of Ale Act 1495 gave powers to local Justices, only being rescinded in 2003. A further statute, from 1550-51 in the reign of Edward VI, imposed new restrictions on what could and could not legally be done in alehouses and tippling houses and, for the first time, required all alehouses to be licensed with a surety of £5 being levied. It was found, in 1577, that England had 329 taverns, 1631 inns and a staggering 14,202 alehouses (though inns did not need licences until 1727). [10]

Meanwhile, in Wharfedale James Ryther, lord of the manor of Harewood, was at work in his characteristically devious and self-seeking way. Beset with personal and financial problems, and destined to end his days in The Fleet debtors' prison, he became one of the many local informers who kept Lord Burghley, Elizabeth's Chief Minister, abreast of what was happening in the provinces. [11] He wrote nine letters to Burghley, most of them damning of Yorkshire folk, high born and low. In one, in 1588, he reported that the 'sises of bred and drynk ar not kept that I can see in any parts of the [county]'. He had already told Burghley, in a letter dated 7 August 1587, that 'many inconvenyencys arise ... by many alehouses, those many and needless alehowses by an evell use of taking money for licences ... [thereby] doubleth the requisite nombre'. Here, he was attacking the justices for their corrupt ways. On 26 January 1588 he wrote on the '... importing matter for the suppressing of our inordynat numbers of typling houses [and] excessive nombres of thes brothel howses'. Here he attacked everyone. He also made the incredible accusation that 'Their ale is in many placis myngled with rosyn [resin] to make yt stronge, in som parts with vryn [urine!]'. How much of this was fact and how much the product of his fawning is impossible to deduce.

In October 1607 two Catterick innkeepers were summoned to appear at the Quarter Sessions in Richmond and each was fined 20s for 'breaking the assize of ale'. [12]

Matters were noticeably tightened by a Royal Proclamation of 1619 which increased the financial commitment needed to obtain or renew a licence to a recognisance of £10 and two sureties of £5, hefty sums in those days. Strict rules were laid down on pricing; alehouse keepers were banned from selling tobacco (that was blatant class discrimination); and they could only serve ale by 'the Ale quarte and not by Jugges or cuppes' – this was to prevent short measures being served.

An official ale measure tankard from 1702, found during excavation of a lime kiln from that period at Ingleton. [13]
(© Ingleborough Archaeology Group)

The 1619 Proclamation also banned 'unlawful' or 'sinful' games in or outside alehouses: dice, cards, backs (backgammon), shovegroat (a precursor to shove ha'penny) and skittles were all outlawed indoors while morris and maypole dancing were forbidden outside. This was nothing new, though, as they had originally been proscribed by Statute in 1326. Alehouse keepers could no longer serve 'rogues, vagabonds, sturdy beggars' or those of ill repute, which must have cut down their customer base. During times of 'divine service they were only allowed to sell ale to travellers and the sick. A paine (a judgement) was laid down in the manor of Giggleswick, in 1564, to the effect that '... noe Alehousekeeper shall keepe in their house any person or persons eateing or drinking in time of Divine Service ...' on paine of 6s 8d payable by the keeper and the same amount by each customer. At that time 6s 8d (half a mark) was a lot of money. Keepers were likewise banned from serving anyone after 9 pm, children at any time and no single person for more than one hour per day.

The poet William Blake had something to say about the respective benefits of being in a pub or going to church. In the first verse of his four-stanza 1794 poem, 'The Little Vagabond', he wrote:

Dear Mother, Dear Mother, the Church is cold,
But the Ale-house is healthy & pleasant & warm;
Besides I can tell where I am use'd well,
Such usage in heaven will never do well

Amen to that, despite the poem's lack of linguistic purity.

The reasoning behind banning games, and the gambling that often accompanied them, was rooted in religious belief and moral ideas. At the moral level, such practices were associated with the 'seedy allure of tavern culture ... gambling, drinking and violence'; at the religious level, with the Betrayal of Christ. [14]

How successful was this Proclamation? One indication is that in 1627 another edict was issued imposing a fine of 20s or a sound whipping on unlicensed alehouse keepers; and in 1638 a tally across the West Riding recorded about 2000 licensed alehouses and an estimated 500 unlicensed! A local alehouse keeper, Henry Procter of Kilnsey, Upper Wharfedale, fell foul of the law in 1641 and was called to answer at a sitting of the West Riding Quarter Sessions in Knaresborough on 5 October. He was described in court as a 'man of contentious and troublesome course of life' and was guilty of 'divers and other misdemeanours' as he kept 'a disorderly alehouse or tippling house to the great disquiet and disturbance of the ... inhabitants'. The court banned him from brewing or selling ale or beer and from keeping a 'commercial ale or tippling house' for three years. Such was his level of contrition and compliance, though, that he appeared again before the end of that same year at a sitting in Wakefield accused of selling ale without a licence. Rules, seemingly, are made to be broken: Procter did it with panache. Maybe he had come to the conclusion that the profits accrued from selling ale outweighed the costs of any likely fines.

In Reeth, in 1666, a local man was summoned before the court for 'allowing divers persons to remain tippling in his house on the Sabbath': this was presumably an alehouse; while a man from Lund Head in Mallerstang was indicted in 1673 for keeping an unlicensed alehouse. [15] Presumably he assumed that being so remote from anywhere was protection enough from the law. Furthermore, in 1690 court records for one manor in eastern Westmorland listed fifty-nine alehouse keepers hauled before the court for evading excise duty and the same names appear time and again. (Jumping forward to 1773 for a moment, across England there was on average one licensed alehouse to every eighty people; and how many unlicensed, one wonders.)

We saw earlier that the predilection of Anglo-Saxon clergy for indulging in alehouse hospitality led to laws being enacted to stop it. It will come as no surprise to learn that the practice and attempts to stamp it out endured for centuries. Edicts from the reign of Henry VIII tried to bring to an end scandalous clerical activities like 'tavern hunting' and the 'playing of dice'; and an item in the Chester Diocesan Visitation records for 1595-96 censured the incumbent at Ingleton for diverse misdemeanours, one of which was that 'ther curate hath kept a Typlynge hous'. Not only did he indulge in drinking, he also provided the means for others to join him in doing so. [16]

In 1711 a sitting of the ecclesiastical court in York heard a case against Stephen Procter to remove him from his position as school master at Kirkby Malham grammar school. [17] He was charged with drunkenness, abusive behaviour, negligence and cruelty, and with refusing to leave his post after being dismissed. The court record is explicit: he was 'much addicted to Drunkenness frequenting of Alehouses and Tipling Houses and have been frequently soe much overtaken with strong Drink ...' that he was wont to rant, rave, holler and shout in the streets and expose his nakedness. Whoever would have thought that could happen in Malhamdale.

Throughout the medieval and early post-medieval centuries clergy were 'notorious for their carousing: they gambled, carried knives, fought in taverns and fraternized with prostitutes'. A twelfth-century law laid down penalties against priests who were found to 'practise drunkenness' or behave as a 'gleeman or tavern-minstrel'. In Elizabethan times the local priest even kept an alehouse 'for honest resort' in Kettlewell, Upper Wharfedale. But why did they persist in behaving in such ways? Selling ale to add to their church's coffers was one thing, but getting drunk quite a different matter.

This might be an appropriate point at which to ponder why people (mostly men, inevitably) felt drawn to alehouses, inns and tippling houses. For some it was the need to find sustenance for an overnight stay away from home; for others a place to discuss business dealings and to complete transactions, whether *bona fide* or illicit; for some this meant engaging in seditious discussions and plotting: anecdotally, the original *Harts Head* in Giggleswick is said to have hosted a coterie of local Jacobites either side of 1700. Other people merely wished to socialise with like-minded people, to relax; while for others on a journey the inn or alehouse was a refuge in the event of storms or impassable fords.

The original Harts Head, Giggleswick

We can look to the memorandum books of a mid-eighteenth century wool frizzer from Wakefield, John Brearley, for a contemporary view. [18] In them he made all manner of comments and observations, whether from first-hand experience or from hearsay, and he was patently anti-drink, quietly railing against over-indulgence. At one point in 1762 he wrote down a verse about the generic man who downs one more drink at an alehouse before 'hee reformed himself'', dedicating his ditty to his glass of Napey ale: [19]

Gett thee from mee
Thou hast undone mee
Yett come to mee for I love thee
Thou hast made my friends my foes
Thou has made me go with tread bare cloaths
But if I get thee to my nose
Then off thou goes.

From medieval times women had a key role in running alehouses, not in a sleazy way, but in a positive way: at least (rural) widows had. From early days they were deemed to be 'deserving paupers' with scant opportunities to earn a living other than by brewing and selling ale, especially if their late husband had been an innholder or alehouse keeper. This tradition, or custom, endured into early-modern times, as evidenced by probate wills and inventories. [20] In 1718 Thomas Carr, a Settle butcher, willed that his 'well beloved wife', Agnes, was to 'keep a publicke and follow the Ale Trade', in his house between his death and the time when his eldest son, Allen, came of age. In 1730 Ann Hargraves of Settle, described as 'widow and Inn Keeper' made her will; and in 1738 William Hall, also of Settle, willed that his wife, Margaret, must 'carry on the Business of an Innholder which we now use'. In 1822-23, for example, across the North Riding part of the National Park eight licences were issued to women: whether or not they were widows was not registered. [21]

Moving on chronologically from the 1619 Proclamation, various Acts were passed all of which tried to impose what previous ones had failed to do. Rationalisation of all existing legislation was the purpose of the 1822 Licensing Act and the Alehouse Act 1828, but the Beer Act 1830 liberalised the brewing and selling of beer partly, perhaps, as the desperate attempt of a very unpopular government to curry favour among the voting cohort. One immediate (inevitable?) impact of this law was a mushrooming in the number of beer-houses (for in-house consumption) and beer-shops (take-aways) as the only condition imposed was a licence fee of two guineas; another, an increase in drunkenness as beer-houses could now serve cheap beer for eighteen hours a day. One unintended (equally inevitable?) consequence was a sharp decline in the number of pre-existing alehouses and inns which could not compete with the new cut-price kids on the block. Another unintended consequence was the number of beer-houses that eventually took the name *King William IV* – it was enacted in his reign and for this reason his popularity ratings soared among dedicated drinkers. Anyone paying the fee could turn their own house into a beer-house as long as they erected a board outside with their own name. For this reason, especially in the North of England, countless beer-houses became known as *The Board,* though this name seems to have first appeared after the passing of the 1822 Act. Many quite soon either went out of business or became beer-houses or public houses dropping the name and adopting a more personalised name. *The Dog and Partridge* in Tosside started life as *The Board*; Settle's *Crown* was *The Board* up to c. 1835; and the *Foresters Arms* in Carlton in Coverdale was *The Board* until at least 1856. Hawes still has a pub called *The Board.* Others across the Dales can be found in contemporary trade directories.

In 1822-23 licences were issued to applicants in eight settlements in the North Riding part of the National Park, all called *Board,* with three separate premises in Middleham all called *Board*; in 1828-29 the numbers had risen to thirteen including two in Carlton in Coverdale.

Yet another consequence was the growth of the mass anti-alcohol Temperance Movement with the rise of Temperance Hotels, Bands of Hope and the Rechabites, among others. Amen to that.

The King William IV, High Street, Settle

*The William IV Public House,
Water Street, Skipton.
It lost its licence after 1908.
(Reproduced by kind permission
of the Ellwood family, Mrs V. Rowley,
and North Yorkshire County
Council, Skipton Library
www.rowleycollection.co.uk)*

What goes round usually comes around and further Acts of 1869, 1872 and 1902 rowed back on the liberalities and excesses of the 1822, 1828 and 1830 Acts, and progressively more small and less viable premises shut down or had their licence renewals refused. The Intoxicating Liquor Act 1914 was dramatic in the scale of its new controls: much reduced opening hours, increased tax on beer, reduced strength of beer, and a ban on buying 'rounds'. A slightly later ordinance banned 'perpendicular drinking', that is standing rather than being seated which had been a strong feature of beer-houses. The national (recorded) rates of drunkenness, however, plummeted by an impressive 600 per cent. During the Great War, of course, so many men were away at the front or on other war duties that the numbers spending long hours in pubs inevitably declined.

We have seen some of the reasons why people frequented alehouses three centuries ago. A wonderfully graphic account of the situation in the 1930s was provided by a government-sponsored mass observation programme. [22] Observers were despatched to pubs in a 'typical working class' town in the North of England; the town was meant to be kept secret. Do not tell anyone, but it was Bolton, which in 1849 had 117 inns, 1888 licensed beer-houses, fifteen unlicensed and twenty where 'thieves and prostitutes resort'. Apart from sitting in a corner and making copious notes, the observers asked customers why they were there. Just over a half claimed that drinking beer was of benefit to their health, probably reflecting advertisements of the time which assured them beer was a 'healthy appetizing drink that will help keep you fit'.

The observers were required to note down what men (them again) actually did in the pub: 'sit and or stand, drink, talk, think, smoke, play games, bet, sing, sell, buy bootlaces and hot pies, black puddings and embrocation' – all reasonable activities, one might argue – and at regular intervals 'shoot tidy gobs of spittle across into the sawdust'. No comment. Now, how did the observers distinguish between a man deep in thought from one in a drunken stupor?

Chapter 2

Alehouses

Many rural alehouses did not have a formal name and it is hard to pin them down unless they gained notoriety or were recorded in, for example, accounts of droving or shown on historical maps. Skellgill (SD923 915), for instance, a tiny settlement west of Askrigg on what is now a dead-end lane, had three hedge alehouses serving packhorse men keen to avoid the tolls on the Askrigg-Sedbergh turnpike road, created in 1761, but which buildings they were cannot be confirmed.

Examples of early alehouses and monastic spitals can be recognised in today's landscape mainly by place-names.

Spittle Croft, Litton

Spittle Croft (SD901 740) in Littondale has long been derelict as a dwelling but the name preserves its origins as a spital for Fountains Abbey's far-flung estate in Littondale.

Lainger House, Bordley

At the southern end of Bordley township, at the junction of former east-west and north-south routes, again on Fountains land, stands a farmstead called Lainger House (SD951 627). The name derives from the Old English word *lengan* which meant to lengthen or prolong, indicative perhaps of a place where people could find succour and accommodation.

High Birkwith, Horton in Ribblesdale

Also at the end of what is now a dead-end road, High Birkwith farm (SD800 768) in Upper Ribblesdale stands where two major medieval routes from north to south – from Dentdale via Thorns and along Cam Road via Ling Gill - were joined by another medieval route, called Langstrothdale Road coming over Greenfield from Upper Wharfedale. High Birkwith, too, was a monastic estate belonging to Jervaulx Abbey and this site is said to have served as a spital and later as an alehouse.

Dry Load, Horton in Ribblesdale

On Cam Road, less than 1000m north of High Birkwith, is a barn now called Dry Lathe but formerly Dry Lade or Dry Lode (SD802 778). The foundation ruins adjacent to the barn were once a farmstead that brought in extra income as a bait-house. The parish registers for Horton in Ribblesdale, for 3 October 1742, record the baptism of Ann, daughter of William Sidgwick of *Dry Load*, innkeeper. It can certainly never have been as grand as an inn though.

St Simon's Chapel, Coverdale

The long-ruined Chapel of St Simon and St Jude, on the south bank of the River Cover at East Scrafton (SE086 849), is first recorded in 1328 but was ruinous by

1582 having fallen foul of Edward VI's passion for abolishing chantry chapels. In 1586, however, an obviously enterprising individual was operating an alehouse – most likely a bait-house – within part of the chapel.

Arkleside bait-house, Coverdale

Coverdale was an important routeway from medieval times onwards connecting Coverham Abbey and Middleham Castle with their estates around Kettlewell in Upper Wharfedale. There were also routes over the moors from West Scrafton and Arkleside southwards and from Horsehouse and Braidley northwards. A building in Arkleside, now residential, was a bait-house at the foot of the pass over to Nidderdale. [23] It has a datestone bearing 'TH 1684 IH' and a wealth of historical architectural detail for such a small building. All the Coverdale settlements had alehouses catering for travellers, packmen and local coal miners such as from Fleensop Colliery to the west.

Kings Head, Horsehouse

Horsehouse (SE047 813), in Coverdale, had two bait-houses and later two inns, one of which gained notoriety for nefarious goings on. The jury is still out but one of the alehouse keepers here may have been responsible for murder: on 30 May 1728 it was reported in the Middlesmoor Township Book that three headless bodies had been discovered in peat up on the moors, close to the road over from Horsehouse, reputedly just three of twenty-five men murdered by a local female 'innkeeper' and her daughter, according to local legend. No one was ever charged with the murders. The near end of the building, with a 1712 date, on the right of this image was the *Kings Head Inn,* shown as such on the 1848-53 OS map.

Jenkin Gate, Oxnop

Even as late as the 1890s vast droves of cattle and sheep were driven southwards over the Stang from the Greta valley in Durham and over Tan Hill from Stainmore. Many droves from both directions took the high level routes from Swaledale to the Askrigg Hill cattle fairs. At the point where the route south from Muker entered the open moor at *Jenkin Gate* (SD931 959) above Oxnop there was an alehouse – probably a bait-house – which survives now as just a field barn but which has signs in its fabric of a much older building. It would also have catered for packhorse men and local lead miners.

Lilly Jock's, Arkengarthdale

The road over the Stang met the Arkengarthdale road at Eskeleth and close to the junction is a long building, now dwellings, that was for many years an alehouse called *Lilly Jock's* (NZ999 034). It is known to have been a drover's 'inn', was used by innumerable packmen, and was marked as a hostelry on an 1836 map of the Tan Hill to Reeth turnpike.

The Drovers, Gunnerside

Another north-south routeway crossed the endless moorland between Tan Hill and Gunnerside in Swaledale. High above Gunnerside Beck lies the straggling hamlet of Winterings where weary travellers could break their journey before dropping down into Swaledale or heading upwards. This image shows the northernmost building in the hamlet which is by far the best candidate to have been *The Drovers,* an alehouse (SD949 994). Now a sad ruin, there is clear structural evidence of a steep thatched roof, a seventeenth-century mullioned window and a much earlier plinth along the south frontage, fireplaces upstairs and down, an external cold store and two stone staircases, one within and one above the cold store: this suggests more than a mere farmhouse.

Crook Seal, Birk Dale

In its own way, equally remote is *Crook Seal* (later Crook Seat, NY836 021) in Birk Dale on the age-old route from Kirkby Stephen to Swaledale. Unoccupied as a dwelling since the middle of the nineteenth century and also with mullioned windows, sixteenth-century evidence and eighteenth-century extensions, it was an important alehouse – or even a simple inn – on this lonely route.

High Dyke, Mallerstang

Prior to the establishment of the turnpike road through Mallerstang in 1765, the main routeway from the Dales to Kirkby Stephen ran high up on the fells to the east of the valley along a route that has variously been termed The High Way or Lady Anne's Highway. At each end there was a challenging ascent or descent and in adverse weather the journey was hazardous. Part way along it lie the ruins of *High Dyke* (SD802 942), a small bait-house that served drovers, packmen and travellers in need of a meal, a drink or two and an overnight doss. It was still in use in this way in 1877, shorter than the turnpike and toll free.

Interior of High Dyke

As an example of a remote hedge alehouse complex High Dyke is unsurpassed, but the range of buildings as seen here emphasises just how basic hedge alehouses were. At the forefront of the image is a single-storey, sixteenth-century building looking towards the two-storey eighteenth-century extension.

Burlington Thwaite, Ribblehead

Another early and long-lived long-distance routeway ran from Dentdale over the eastern flanks of Whernside as the Craven Way before heading south-west along the base of the hill as Kirkby Gate. This route would have taken travellers through the hamlet of Winterscales past the *Burlington Thwaite* (SD754 801) near Ribblehead. Surviving now as a small ruinous outbuilding and foundations, this has been called a 'wayside inn' [24] but, again, it would just have been a hedge alehouse.

High Barn, Twisleton

The original name of this former bait-house is unknown but High Barn (SD713 754), below Chapel-le-Dale, still has a fireplace on the ground and former first floors and the corbelled chimney is visible in this view. It, too, has been grandiosely described as an inn. [25]

Dale Head, Stainforth

The network of packhorse and drove routes spread across the Dales and yet another important and ageless north-south route ran from Wensleydale past Semer Water, over the moors between Raydale and Deepdale on a now-lost route, then across Horse Head Pass to Halton Gill in Littondale and between Fountains Fell and Pen-y-ghent to Stainforth (where the present *Craven Heifer* changed its name from *The Packhorse* c. 1837). At the head of Littledale is *Dale Head* (SD840 716), once a bait-house with small enclosures where ponies could be let loose overnight.

Stubbins, Threshfield

One of the most well known and well-trodden medieval routeways, vital to the management of Fountains Abbey's vast estates in Upper Wharfedale and on Malham Moor, was Mastiles Lane, part of the monastic Road of Lonsdall. One of its eastern branches led up what are now Hard Gate and Malham Moor Lane; at Skirethorns where it begins to climb in earnest there was the inevitable hedge alehouse or bait-house, now called Stubbings Laithe (SD977 640). One story tells us that it was at *Stubbins* 'public-house' (pedantically, it wasn't a public house) a keeper's daughter was murdered by her boyfriend because she had been unfaithful to him. [26] It is said that on every 2nd January a pool of blood can be seen outside – but at what time? It had gone out of use by the middle of the nineteenth century at the latest.

Great Close House, Malham Moor

At Malham Tarn there is a vast enclosure called Great Close, almost 300 ha (c. 730 acres) in extent. It was subdivided in modern times but from 1745 to at least 1786 the entire area was rented by John Birtwhistle, one of the greatest cattle dealers in the North, and a local man. Initially, he (and his predecessors) held autumn cattle fairs here when countless numbers of cattle driven from Scotland were fattened up and sold to dealers or other drovers from further south. It was inevitable that vast quantities of ale would be supped and food consumed, stories and gossip exchanged, and probably scores settled. Where else to do all this than in an alehouse? *Great Close House* (SD905 665), a long four-bay building, was the main alehouse during fairtime.

Lone Head, Bordley

As time went on Great Close was relegated to a ground where livestock – sheep and cattle – were fattened up, for as long as three weeks, before being sold with the centre of dealing transferred to Boss Moor between Bordley and Threshfield. Here, *Lone Head* alehouse served the insatiable needs of the drovers and dealers (SD955 631). What was left of the building was demolished very recently.

Lone Head cold store

In the paddock adjacent to the former alehouse this recently collapsed structure was a cold store. It runs into the banking and has side chambers with intact stone shelving where food and provisions were kept cool.

Chapter 3

Wayside and Village Inns

Over the past century or so the term 'inn' has become rather meaningless and today there is a tendency to call an establishment an 'inn' as a sales ploy designed to evoke a mythical and romanticised view of what inns used to be. It is also common today to see them advertised as the '... Inn Hotel', which is a contradiction; even in the mid-nineteenth century some inns were already relabelled hotel. *The Golden Lion Inn* in Settle, for instance, was advertised as the *Golden Lion Hotel* long before the end of that century.

In the past there was a spectrum of inns. At the apex of the hierarchy were the 'Christmas card' coaching inns with mail coaches, stage coaches and post chaises and (generally) high standards of service. Bear in mind, though, that the mail coach concept was only conceived in 1784, and the heyday of the coaching inn lasted only two decades, from the 1820s to the 1840s, before being killed off by growth in the rail network. These inns were sited on major long-distance routes. Below them in the hierarchy were inns on lesser but still important routes, often not turnpike roads. Yet others took advantage of major livestock fairs held on long-distance routes which, unlike alehouses, offered a higher level of service and catered for passing trade as well. Then there were inns within villages attending to passing trade, visitors and local needs: some of these were little more than glorified public houses, others were coaching inns. Kettlewell in Upper Wharfedale, for example, had five inns and a beer-house in 1838 – but how many of the inns really were inns? [27] One contemporary account of Malhamdale noted that Malham had 'a comfortable [unnamed] Public House' that did not offer 'the luxuries of life' but did provide 'attention and a rural fare'. [28] On the other hand, a rather later commentator there was less enthusiastic writing '... we soon became disgusted with our inn'. [29] Again, the inn was not named. As discussed earlier, many inns fell on hard times after the Beer Act 1830 and the advent of rail travel. This chapter looks at examples from each of these four categories.

Cross Streets, Austwick

Long before what is now the A65 was turnpiked in 1753, the main route from Leeds via Skipton and Settle ran through Giggleswick and Lawkland and then Austwick. The new turnpike road crossed this older route at the obvious point to establish an inn: after all, older routes were preferred by those who objected to paying turnpike tolls. The inn was (appropriately) called *Cross Streets* (SD772 675), though not universally. As with so many rural inns, in 1861 the innkeeper, Thomas Scott, also farmed 37 ha (92 acres). Trade directories and census records list it as the *Joiner's Arms* from 1838-61 and 1877-81; it did not appear on the list of licensed premises for 1828. The 1871 and 1891 censuses have it as *Cross Streets Inn* and *Cross o' Streets Inn* respectively. This postcard, dating from c. 1910 when Richard Lord was proprietor, shows it as Cross Streets Hotel. It closed down c. 2002. *(Author's collection)*

Red Lion, Bolton Abbey

An equally obvious place to site an inn was at a river crossing, especially where two townships met. Parish constables were responsible for keeping the peace and for keeping an eye on hostelries. It was widely accepted that their jurisdiction ran thin at such boundaries so they were most unlikely to call in on border inns, especially if it involved a considerable journey from their home base. Thus, the *Red Lion Inn* (SE073 529,) on the east side of the River Wharfe at Bolton Bridge, was ideally placed to catch passing trade while avoiding the glare of the constable. It has a known history from 1850-90, was likely not there much earlier than that, and had gone out of use by 1907. One account, from 1850, noted that the inn had 'less *(sic)* pretensions where cheapness, rural fare, and civility may be had'. [30]

The Bull, Mallerstang

Partway down Mallerstang two routes merged – one was the old route upgraded as the Sedbergh to Kirkby Stephen turnpike in 1825, the other an equally old but high-level route, now a byway called Hellgill Wold, that dropped down from Hellgill Bridge to Shaw Paddock. This farm was also an inn – initially *The Bull* but later *Shaw Paddock* (SD785 952) – serving travellers and, especially, cattle drovers on their southbound journey. While the Settle-Carlisle railway was under construction in the 1870s it would also have served as a pub and lodging house for navvies. It is thought to have given up or lost its licence around 1900.

Cock and Guns, Garsdale Head

The original Askrigg to Sedbergh turnpike of 1761 followed Old Road from Garsdale Head to Raygill. At the top of a steep section of road called Cock Brow stands the substantial but long-derelict *Cock and Guns Inn* (SD772 909). It was mentioned in a probate inventory of 1733 and was still operative in 1873 while the 1892-93 OS map marked it as a house rather than an inn. It is surprising it lasted so long as the turnpike road was realigned to the present course of the A684 in 1825 cutting off much of its passing trade. Its name suggests it hosted shooting parties as well as travellers.

George and Dragon, Garsdale

Some 3 km further down Garsdale stands the semi-derelict Garsdale Hall (SD745 895), an impressive range comprising hall, barn and granary with a coach house across the road. This served as an inn – the *George and Dragon* – for many years though the 1848 OS map does not name it as such. It has the appearance of having been a 'proper' high-status inn.

Brewhouse at Halfpenny House, Barden

The Richmond to Lancaster turnpike of 1751 took a course south of the River Swale, on what is now a minor road through Brokes and across Barden Fell then over Bellerby and Leyburn Moors towards Askrigg. At a five-way junction – significantly on the Barden-Bellerby-Walburn township boundary – *Halfpenny House* Farm was for many years known as *Hutton's House* (SE127 950). Opposite the farm complex is the former brewhouse, with one kneeler bearing the inscription 'BREWHOUSE' and the other '1832'. As seen in the image, the stairs and door in the gable end gave access to the upper floor, and the recess in the roadside wall gave access to the pure waters of a spring that enabled the brewhouse to work efficiently. This was a well known drovers' inn and the 'halfpenny' element in its name most probably relates to the drover's overnight grazing charge per beast or the cost per head of road tolls. It is listed in the extant North Riding Quarter Sessions registers from 1775 to 1829 and was named as the Halfpenny House Public House on 1854 OS maps. In 1840 Charles Mason was the licensee; in 1897 it was said that it had been an inn until '30 years ago', [31] but William Spence was named as licensee in an 1890 trade directory.

Slip Inn, Leyburn

Further west on the same turnpike, on what is now referred to as the Tank Road, lies a former farmstead called Deer Park (SE096 927). Little is known of its life as the *Slip Inn* other than it was operational in 1857 but not in 1891. The house itself is not old so it may have been a short-lived venture.

Bridge Inn, Middleham

Middleham lay on a historical main route ultimately connecting London with Richmond and travel north of the town required a crossing of the River Ure. Middleham Low Moor was the venue for one of the major livestock fairs and untold numbers of cattle converged on the crossing into the late nineteenth century. Until 1829 there was no bridge; in 1830 the new iron suspension bridge collapsed under the weight of an unruly drove; it was replaced in 1831 and on the Middleham side *Bridge Inn* (SE119 887) was built to serve travellers ... and to collect tolls for crossing the bridge. The present bridge is a later rebuild; the inn served its last customers in 1856.

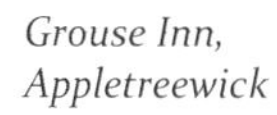

Grouse Inn, Appletreewick

On the Pateley Bridge to Grassington turnpike road, created in 1758, almost exactly halfway between the two market towns, travellers as well as local nineteenth-century lead miners could take advantage of the *The Grouse* (SE080 633) at Dry Gill. In 1849 it was *The Grouse Public House*, in 1889 and 1907 the *Grouse Inn.*

YORKSHIRE.

HIGHLY VALUABLE FREEHOLD PROPERTY

Situate at Carlton, near Skipton, in Craven.

TO BE SOLD BY AUCTION,

By Messrs Hardwick & Best,

At the Devonshire Hotel, in Skipton,

ON WEDNESDAY, THE 25th, DAY OF JULY, next,

At two o'clock in the afternoon, subject to such conditions as will be then & there produced,

A VERY VALUABLE

FREEHOLD ESTATE

Situate in the Township and Parish of Carlton, near the Market Town of Skipton, in the picturesque and interesting District of Craven, in the West Riding of the County of York, consisting of a MESSUAGE or DWELLING HOUSE, called the AIREDALE INN, with the adjoining Outbuildings and appurtenances situate in the Village of Carlton, and several closes of highly cultivated and rich Meadow, Pasture, and Arable Land, containing altogether about 44 acres Statute Measure, which will be offered for Sale in the following or such other Lots as may be agreed upon at the time of Sale, viz.--

LOT 1.

All those two closes of Pasture Land situate on Pinhaw Moor, and adjoining each other, called the "COPY" and the "INTACK" containing respectively in Statute Measure 3a. 0r. 31 and a half perches, and 0a. 2r. 21 and three quarter perches or thereabouts.

LOT 2.

All those two closes of Pasture and Meadow Land, called the "ADDLE CROFT" and "LIVERSTEADS" adjoining each other, and containing respetively in Statute Measure 15a. 1r. 25p. and 1a. 0r. 38p. or thereabouts.

LOT 3.

All that Messuage or Dwelling-House situate in the village of Carlton, now occupied as a Beer-house and known by the name of the "AIREDALE INN" together with the Garden, Barn, Stable, Outbuildings & appurtenances to the same belonging, & the two closes called the "CROFTS" situate behind & adjoining the same containing altogether in Statute Measure 1a. 2r. 38 and a half perches or thereabouts.

LOT 4.

All that Close of arable Land called "Sand Holme" containing in Statute Measure 2a. 1r. 28p. or thereabouts.

LOT 5.

All that close of Pasture Land called "Lower and Far Carla Beck and Moor Flatts" containing in Statute Measure 4a. 1r. 17p. or thereabouts abutting on the high road leading from Skipton to Carlton.

LOT 6.

All those two closes of Meadow and Pasture Land called the "Long Field" and "Broad Ing" adjoining each other containing respectively in Statute Measure 2a. 3r. 34p. and 2a. 2r. 8p. or thereabouts and abutting on Carla Beck Lane.

LOT 7.

All that close of Meadow Land called "Lincoln Flatt" containing in Statute Measure 2a. 2r. 13p. or thereabouts and abutting on the high road leading from Skipton to Carlton.

LOT 8.

All that close of Meadow Land called "Lincoln Flatt Meadow" containing in Statute Measure 1a. 3r. 29 and a half perches or thereabouts, and abutting on Carla Beck Lane aforesaid.

LOT 9.

All that close of Pasture Land with the Water-course, Plantation, and Barn therein called "Carla Beck" containing in Statute Measure 5a. 0r. 2p. or thereabouts, and abutting on Carla Beck Lane aforesaid.

All the Premises are in the occupation of Mr, Job Ellison, as Tenant from year to year. The Land is in a high state of cutivation and well watered and the Buildings and Fences are in good repair. Lots 3, 5, 6, 7, 8 and 9 are especially worthy of the attention of Capitalists as being situate in a pleasant District, adjoining good roads, & within a short distance, (less than a mile) from the Skipton Station, of the Midland Railway, & they command very beautiful & extensive views of the surrounding country & afford excellent sites for the erection of ornamental villas & country residences,

The Tenant Mr. Job Ellison will shew the premises, and Lithographed Plans and Printed Particulars of the Estate with further Information may be obtained at the Offices of Messrs. Cowgill and Knight, Land Agents, &c., Bradford; of Messrs. Hardwick and Best, the Auctioneers; and of

Mr. GEORGE HARTLEY, Solicitor, Settle,

Plans and Particulars are left at the Devonshire Hotel, in Skipton, at the Airedale and Swan Inns, in Carlton, and at the other Principal Inns, in the District.

Settle, 16th June, 1855.

JOHN WILDMAN, PRINTER, NEW STREET, SETTLE.

Airedale Inn, Carleton in Craven 1855

Grundy Farm at Carleton (SD974 497), near Skipton, was a farm from at least 1615/16 but two centuries later it operated as a beer-house known as the *Airedale Inn* and in 1855 was let to Job Ellison, farmer and drover. *(Author's collection)*

Airedale Inn

The fact that it lay on a major east-west packhorse and drove route, connecting Skipton and Colne, suggests that it had been an inn that slipped down the scale as a result of the 1828 and 1830 Acts. Its fine roadside façade supports the contention that it had been a significant inn. It was not listed in the 1822 Quarter Sessions records or mentioned in county-wide trade directories of 1826-67; by 1885 there was no reference to it as a beer-house but it was still owned by cattle dealers, as it had been for over a hundred years.

Greenwell, Dentdale

Also lying at a cross-roads of packhorse routes where Deepdale meets Dentdale is *Greenwell* (SD714 862), now a farm but said to have been a wayside inn called by that name. It was not marked as such on 1848 or 1892 OS maps so had presumably lost its hospitality function before then which would make sense as turnpikes and railways were inexorably killing off the packhorse trade.

Travellers Rest, Calvert Houses

Calvert Houses is a small hamlet lying on a high road that was once a long-distance route from Kirkby Stephen via Keld, Arn Gill and Ivelet Side to Calvert Houses and the rest of Swaledale. It also lay close to a significant lead-mining area. *The Travellers Rest* (SD926 980) was opened at Calvert Houses as a hostelry to serve both travellers and miners. The 1841 census listed one farming family resident here and eight mining families. The 1854 OS map did not mark it as a hostelry; it was named in an 1890 trade directory with Ralph Harker as licensee, and an 1891-92 edition showed it as a public house, but by 1898 it had closed down. Either it had a very short life as a pub – but why here? – or it had operated for who knows how long under another name: it was probably the *Board*.

Slip Inn, Gayles

Another main route led from Richmond north-westwards through the village of Gayles on the edge of the Yorkshire Dales towards Bowes in County Durham. Just east of the village the *Slip Inn* (NZ129 071), later Slip Inn Farm, was a small wayside inn offering basic accommodation to travellers. It would have been more than an alehouse but by no means in the upper league of inns. In 1890 William Anderson ran the inn.

Gearstones Inn, Ribblehead

Gearstones Inn (SD780 800) was a prime example of an inn that tapped into three markets – passing travellers, grouse-shooting parties and those attending the periodic cattle fairs and butter markets. It has a long recorded history with the first substantive document being a Conditions of Sale Notice dated 10 May 1817. It was advertised as an 'inn or public house ... with five good rooms' on the ground floor, cellars, 'fine excellent Lodging Rooms' on the upper floor, an attic, two barns, a chaise house, stables with a hay chamber over, a 'good Cottage', brewhouse, offices, gardens and farmland. [32] It had been in the Lister family's ownership for many generations but on William's death it was put up for sale and was bought by Oliver Farrer, lord of the manor of Newby and joint owner of the Ingleborough Estate. The inn was rebuilt in the 1880s but, as the Farrers were keen on developing their estate as a prime grouse shooting concern, in 1911 they closed the inn down to use it as a shooting lodge. *(Ref. no. b12939, © and courtesy The Shaw Collection at Blackburn with Darwen Library and Information Service)*

Gearstones

The Hon. John Byng, later 5th Viscount Torrington, undertook the obligatory aristocratic grand tour of these islands between 1781 and 1794, on horseback. In June 1792 he journeyed westwards from Bainbridge in weather he described as 'feels November ... so cold, and so rainy ... [with] many storms of rain'. [33] He happened to arrive at Gearstones to overnight while a cattle fair was in progress on the moor just north of the inn. In fact he referred to the inn as a 'moor alehouse' or a public house 'called Grierstones, the seat of misery, in a desert;

and tho' fill'd with company, yet the Scotch fair held upon the heath ... added to the horror of the curious scenery: the ground in front crowded by Scotch cattle and drovers; and the house cramm'd by the buyers and sellers, most of whom were in plaids, filibegs etc ... the only custom of this hotel or rather hovel, is derived from the grouse shooters, or from two Scotch fair; when at the conclusion of the day's squabble the two Nations agree in mutual drunkenness ...' For his stay, with his servant, he paid 1s 4d for food, 1s 9d for drinks and 1s for corn for his horse. His meal consisted of 'boil'd slices of stale pork, and some fry'd eggs, with some wretched beer and brandy:- to which my hunger was not equal; and from which my delicacy revolted'. If only Trip Advisor had existed then.

Another real-life anecdote for Gearstones dates from September 1840 when George Smith, steward to the Hornby Castle Estate near Lancaster, travelled by carriage to Leyburn. He left Wray at 5 am, breakfasted at Gearstones at 8 am, arrived in Hawes at 10 am and Leyburn at 3.15 pm. The whole journey was 65 km (41 miles) and the journey time over ten hours. Howson's Guide, from 1850, found Gearstones a 'comfortable place of rest'.

Newby Head, Ribblehead

On either side of the Pennine watershed, between Ribblesdale and Widdale, at the boundary not just between two townships but formerly between two counties, there was an inn, both established when the Richmond to Lancaster turnpike was diverted from over Cam to the Widdale-Gearstones route in 1795, and both listed as among England's highest inns. *Newby Head Inn* (SD794 840), like so many others also a farm, was described in 1864 as a 'clean, respectfully conducted inn'. It was popular among drovers and not just when the Gearstones fairs were underway. Its licence expired in 1919.

New Widdale Head Inn, Widdale

On the North Riding side of the boundary stood *New Widdale Head Inn* which, for some unknown reason, was preferred by butchers and cattle dealers attending the fairs, not to mention travellers. A letter of recommendation, dated 28 August 1841, was written to the authorities in respect of applications for licence renewal by the two competing inns – Newby Head and Widdale Head. [34] One Hammond submitted 'a most numerously and respectably signed memorial' stating the 'fitness of Widdale Head as a House of good accommodation for travellers', a memorial whose signatories included 'several clergymen, gentlemen travellers and many drovers of cattle'. The 1848 OS map marked it as a public house, and it was still licensed in 1885 but its date of closure is unknown.

Bull and Cave, Clapham

Most villages had at least one inn, to cater for local people and those on business plus visitors to the area. After 1830, as discussed earlier, many slid down the ladder to become pubs.

Clapham held annual livestock fairs which drew in huge numbers of thirsty people; it lay on the original line of the Keighley to Kendal turnpike and, prior to that, was on a medieval highway from Lancaster through Bentham and where another early road (now the Pennine Bridleway) branched off over the tops to Selside and beyond. From about 1760 it was also the seat of the Farrers, owners of the vast Ingleborough Estate with its shooting emphasis. The village had six inns and public houses in the late eighteenth and nineteenth centuries: several were purchased by the Farrers. One of them was the *Bull and Cave Inn,* now offices. A tourist guide from 1850 recommended two inns here, of which this was one. Apart from bringing in visitors for a grouse-shooting spree, the estate was also keen to promote Ingleborough Cave as a tourist destination, after 1837, and it needed good accommodation. The *Old Black Bull Inn* was named in trade directories in 1822 and 1838, and in Quarter Sessions records for 1828, as well as on the 1847 tithe apportionment map whereas the Bull and Cave was not recorded before 1847. According to a clipping from an unknown local newspaper, by 1877 the Farrers had shut down both of these inns (as well as the *Red Lion* and a beershop) leaving just the *New Inn.*

Bridge Inn, Ingleton

In 1823 the Keighley-Kendal turnpike road was diverted from its original course through the heart of Ingleton and over the two rivers to a new line, the present A65. A new bridge was built across the Greta, complete with new toll house. *The Bridge Inn* was built, before 1828 when it was listed as licensed premises, on the village side of the river. Howson's 1850 guide named it, and the long-since demolished *Bay Horse Inn*, closed down in 1870, as Ingleton's two recommended inns. In 1844 the licensee was a Mr Mattinson; by 1848 his widow ran it. It went out of business in 2003 and was incorporated into a housing development.

Fountain Inn,
Burton in Lonsdale

Burton in Lonsdale was noted from the 1650s to 1944 as a major centre for pottery manufacture, as well as cotton textiles, and, inevitably, potential customers and entrepreneurs were drawn to the village and they needed somewhere to stay. One of Burton's main inns was the *Fountain Inn* on Low Street. Several dates stick out in the sparse record for this inn: then called *Fountainhead*, it was well established in 1767 as it was the meeting house for the Bentham Moor Enclosure commissioners; and on 16 May 1829 an overnight visitor was charged the princely sum of £2 16s 4d for his food and drink, the internal services of a chamber maid and waiter, and the external services of an ostler and 'Boots'. By 1900 its licence had been surrendered.

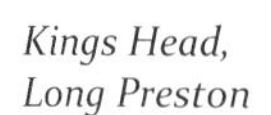

Kings Head,
Long Preston

As we have seen, villages on turnpike (and earlier main) roads invariably had a selection of inns to tempt the passing traveller, or where business arrangements were in place between licensee and coachmen or carriers for midday or overnight stopovers. Long Preston still has two 'inns' and possibly had two more: one of these was the *Kings Head*, at the corner of Church Street. It operated as an inn from the early 1700s to the early 1800s.

Bulls Head, Cracoe

In Upper Wharfedale, at the junction of the 1853 Skipton to Cracoe turnpike and the road westwards, the *Bulls Head Inn* (SD974 599) was one of those inns ideally placed to capture passing trade and serve local needs. When it was founded is not known but it certainly existed in 1822; closure came in 1916, a victim of tightening of the licensing screws during the First World War.

Kirk Yett, Linton

It was not uncommon for parish churches to own inns – this was the case at Hubberholme in Upper Wharfedale and at Linton, formerly the church for a huge area around Grassington. *Kirk Yett* (SE004 632) was recorded as an inn in the seventeenth century but achieved some notoriety – according to local belief – being shut down by the Archdeacon. Apparently the church wardens were wont to spend their time imbibing jugs of ale in the inn rather than a sip of diluted communion wine in the church. Difficult choice.

Spout Yat, Hartlington

This inn in the tiny village of Hartlington, east of Burnsall, has a very shadowy history with no reliably known dates. All that can be said is that it was an inn which probably saw its heyday in the years when neighbouring Appletreewick held its annual Onion Fairs and periodic horse and cattle fairs. *Spout Yat* (SE039 609) fronts onto the road that led to the fairs. Outside the inn a telltale horse mounting block has survived.

Anglers Arms, Kilnsey

The tiny hamlet of Kilnsey in Upper Wharfedale lay on a major route that ultimately connected Halifax with Richmond, passing through Skipton and Kettlewell before climbing over the tops to Coverdale and Middleham. The *Anglers Arms* (SD974 678) is recorded as an inn from 1760 and the building, now a house, bears a datestone HEO 1768, Henry (and Elizabeth?) Ovington, its owners at that time. In 1822 and 1838 it was called the *Anglers Inn*, in 1826 the *Anglers Arms*. From 1851 to 1882 the licensee was John Inman but on his retirement the licence was surrendered by the then owner who also owned the neighbouring *Tennants Arms*. However, it was refurbished and re-opened as *The Old Anglers Arms*. It closed for good in 1930. On the opposite side of the road to the former inn an extant small building was the brewhouse and laundry.

White Lion, Bainbridge

Several routes converged on Bainbridge: an ancient route over Stake Road from Wharfedale, an equally old route up Wensleydale from the east, and the Richmond-Lancaster turnpike. The original turnpike (1751-95) crossed the Ure at Yore Bridge, then the village green before heading up the never-ending drag of Cam High Road. In between this road and the two ancient routes, nestling below the western edge of the Roman fort, was the *White Lion Inn*. If ever an inn was established at an obvious location, this was it. It was operative at least by 1823, when Ann Stockdale was the licensed victualler, and it may well have been conceived in 1751 to benefit from increased footfall on the new turnpike. The fact that it survived after the route was diverted up Widdale means this made no real difference to its viability. In 1840 Richard Trotter was the innholder, it was named on the 1854 OS map but not on the 1891 map, so must have closed between those two years.

Boar Inn, Countersett

At the point before the long haul up Stake Road, the small hamlet of Countersett had an inn – *The Boar(d) Inn* – offering succour to travellers as well as a social gathering place for those who lived around Semer Water. According to the 1892 OS map it was called *Board Inn*; on the 1910 map it was *Boar Inn*: maybe 'Board' was by then deemed to be too reminiscent of an old beer-house. On its front wall is a stone-plaque inscription in Latin, inserted in 1667 by the then owners, Bartholomew and Isabel Harrison, whose initials adorn it. It translates as 'Now it is mine, soon yours, but after that I know not whose'. It was not named in the Quarter Sessions records of 1822-23 or 1828-29 but was named as an inn in a trade directory of 1890. It closed in 1914 – another victim of wartime restrictions.

The George Inn, Askrigg

Little is known of this inn other than that it was operational by 1823 but had closed by 1891. In 1823 Matthew Thompson ran the inn, then known as the *George and Dragon*, as well as pursuing his trade as a slater; in 1840, as *The George*, William Heseltine was licensee. Given its hemmed-in situation, it can never have been more than a second-level inn. Now housing, it is adjacent to the *Crown Inn* at the top of Main Street.

Punch Bowl, Preston-under-Scar

Now in domestic use, the *Punch Bowl Inn* in the centre of the small village of Preston-under-Scar, Wensleydale, was a substantial property with barn and granary at one end serving as an inn and local pub. It was not named on the OS maps of 1854 or 1891 but George Carter was mentioned as licensee from 1792 to 1823, and Thomas Armstrong was victualler here in 1840. [35] By 1890, however, it was probably what a trade directory described as *Temperance Hotel.*

The Star Inn, West Witton

West Witton did not benefit from being on a turnpike road but was on an ancient route up Wensleydale which probably coped with just as much traffic as a turnpike. Four inns fronted the road within the village, two still operative, one long-since disappeared, and one now a guest house – *The Star Inn*. Examining its frontage provides clues to its licensed past: a horse mounting block, a nineteenth-century iron bracket for the name sign and its position set back from the road to allow coaches and chaises to pull off the road. It may have been established in the eighteenth century (or earlier?) and is recorded through the following century. Elizabeth Fairbank ran it between at least 1823 and 1840, and in 1890 E. Graham divided his time between running it and carrying on his trade as a butcher.

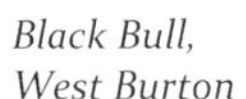

Black Bull, West Burton

Sited on the village green in West Burton, the eighteenth-century *Black Bull Inn* lay at the junction of several historical packhorse routes: south-west through Newbiggin in Bishopdale, south up Waldendale and over Walden Moor to Upper Wharfedale, east over Harland Hill to Carlton in Coverdale, and south-east over Fleensop Moor to Horsehouse and Braidley further up

Coverdale. West Burton also held livestock fairs and was close to several collieries. *(Ref. no. b12947, © and courtesy The Shaw Collection at Blackburn with Darwen Library and Information Service)*

Black Bull

The *Black Bull* is recorded from the early eighteenth century, was listed in the 1822-23 and 1828-29 licensing records, but by 1857 had been downgraded to a public house, still open in 1933 according to a trade directory, but not in 1937. It had the requisite inn's stable block, cellar and mounting block.

Spotted Cow, Newbiggin

Bishopdale's Newbiggin lay on an important east-west packhorse route and an occasional local drove route. It had several bait-houses and inns at one time or another. There is some confusion about names: at the road junction in the village centre stood an inn that was for a time called the *Spotted Cow Inn*. Census records confirm that George Heseltine was innkeeper in Newbiggin from 1851 to 1871 but his inn was not named; the 1881 census records him as publican of the *Heifer Inn*. Was that the *Spotted Cow* or the *Bishopdale Heifer*, named as a public house on OS maps in 1891 and 1910; yet from 1913 to 1925 it was called the *Heifer Inn* but the *Spotted Cow Inn* in 1929. Was the name changed because the name Spotted Cow was perceived in negative ways, or were they two separate properties? Whichever, Heseltine provided for his wife and thirteen children by small-scale farming and by droving cattle from the dale to York, which probably explains his absence from the 1871 census record. An 1840 trade directory named Rebecca Webster as victualler at the *Spotted Cow*. By 1933 it was no longer listed. To add to the confusion, today one house is called Spotted Heifer Cottage.

Moorcock, Carlton in Coverdale

The Moorcock in Carlton, Coverdale, has a long range of buildings with the inn at one end, a coach or trap house in the middle; barn, granary and brewhouse at the opposite end; and a courtyard at the rear. It is unmistakeably a former inn. In fact, it was purpose built c. 1800, with the brewhouse tagged on later. It was not listed as The Moorcock in the Quarter Sessions records for 1822-23 or 1828-29 or in an 1840 trade directory, but it had been yet another *Board Inn* for many years. Its date of closure is known – the 1960s.

The XYZ, Carlton in Coverdale

Carlton for many years supported three establishments, though the innholders were farmers as well. Now Seaton House, the *XYZ Inn* was the first to buckle: it had relied on the droving trade so perhaps the demise of this led to the inn's non-viability. The owner in 1861, William Harrison, gave up innkeeping and converted the building into a mixed grocer's/draper's shop. [36]

The Moorhen, West Scrafton

One inn that is known to have changed its name several times was in the small village of West Scrafton, also in Coverdale. In 1822-23 there was one licensed house here – the *Moor Cock*; in 1828-29 there was just *The Board*; in the 1830s and in 1840 *The Partridge*; then *The Grouse Inn* from the later 1840s to 1890. Only later was there *The Moorhen Inn*. At least, most of them related to game birds! It had a barn, stable, granary, cart or trap house, cowshed, dairy and cellar: it was both farm and inn. Apart from whatever visitors came here, it also served local coal miners and sandstone quarrymen and textile workers. The licence was allowed to lapse in 1925.

The Lady Bab, Coverham

Near Coverham Church, and part of what was later a Cow & Gate dairy, a decaying seventeenth-century house was the *Lady Bab Inn* (SE099 864), named after an early nineteenth-century racehorse, presumably from one of the local stables, and was much frequented by the racing fraternity. It is not listed in either 1822-23 or 1828-29 so may have been so-named later on: both lists only have *The Board* in Coverham township. One of its licensees, James Clifford, was heavily fined for illegally selling alcohol on Middleham Moor. It first appears as *The Lady Bab* in 1890; it closed, as did so many across the country, in 1911.

The Fox and Hounds, East Witton

Also not named in either licensing list was the *Old Holly Tree* in East Witton where Coverdale opens out into Wensleydale: it was, however, named as the *Fox and Hounds* on the 1828-29 licensing list, and in 1823 and 1840 Peggy Buckton was listed as licensee; on the 1849-53 OS map it was marked as 'PH' rather than inn, but there is no doubt from examination of the complex that it was a coaching inn, ideally sited on the main Masham–Leyburn-Richmond road. Its date of closure has not been determined, nor when it began its life but, in 1897, it was noted that East Witton had had two or three inns c. 1800, including the 'picturesque-looking temperance hotel being [in 1800] a fully-licensed house called the *Fox and Hounds*'. [37] On the frontage is a large painted board with the motto *Sic Viresco*: this translates literally as 'Thus I grow green' but more loosely as 'Thus I flourish'. An 1890 trade directory noted only *Temperance Hotel.*

The Good Intent, Richmond

Immediately across Richmond Bridge, in the hamlet of Sleegill, there stands a building – the *Good Intent Inn* – on land once in the possession of St Martin's Priory. The present building is from the late eighteenth century and its iron name-board bracket is still in situ. Apart from attending to the demands of passing travellers, who may have found cheaper lodging here than in Richmond's inns, it also served copper miners who toiled in Billy Bank Wood immediately west of the inn. Yet again, it was not listed in the 1820s records but was depicted on the 1854 OS map as the *Good Intent PH*, so its life as a proper inn must have been short. Mapping from 1891-92 marked only 'PH'; in 1890 William Wright was licensee here as well as being a blacksmith; but mapping from 1911 marked nothing, though it is said to have closed in 1914 – it had been shut down, possibly as mining had ceased by then, or because of wartime restrictions if the latter date is correct.

Farmers Arms, Bellerby

The village of Bellerby north of Leyburn was not on a turnpike road but was on an important link from the town to the Richmond to Lancaster turnpike. On a small lane – The Old Wynd – in the centre of the village, a large imposing house was once the *Farmers Arms*. It has a datestone of 1732, which is in keeping with the building's façade, and that may signal when it began its licensed life; it was not listed in the 1820's records but was named on the 1856 OS map. However, it was not listed in a trade directory from 1890.

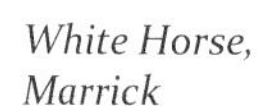

White Horse, Marrick

Another imposing house, this time in the small village of Marrick above Swaledale, has seventeenth-century detail but a date-stone from 1738. It was the *White Horse Inn*, of which little is known for certain, other than that it probably closed down in the 1960s. In 1823 Jane Whaley ran the inn and was also a shopkeeper; in 1840 Susan – Jane's daughter perhaps – was licensee, and in 1890 C. Whitelock was licensee and a butcher. In 1920 Mr and Mrs Ellerton ran the inn. It was a typical quiet rural inn, off the beaten track.

Green Dragon, Hurst

North of Marrick a dead-end road leads to the former and important lead-mining community of Hurst. At the far west end of the settlement was the *Green Dragon Inn* (NZ045 023). It would have catered for visitors to the mine and also slaked the endless thirst of the miners, and no doubt became unviable when mining ceased. It has a date-stone of 1737.

Cat Hole Inn, Keld c. 1900

On the historical route from Kirkby Stephen through Birk Dale to Swaledale, on the southern edge of the village of Keld, the *New Inn* was opened in what was an existing farm complex, again ideally suited to catch passing travellers. The building itself dates from the nineteenth century. At some point after 1848 its name changed to the *Cat Hole Inn* (NY893 008), to commemorate a local waterfall. The 1854 OS map just marks 'PH' so it had clearly been downgraded in status, when it closed its doors for the last time is not known. This photograph is of a group from Reeth Methodist Church on an outing to the inn around 1900. Local anecdote claims that a Methodist intended to buy the inn to close it down: that did happen but not at this time. *(© Swaledale Museum. Image SM 1335).*

Cat Hole Inn This photograph dates from c. 1934. (Copyright the Francis Frith Collection. K66049A)

Manor Inn, Thornton Rust

For some 'lost' inns there is little or no information about their past, other than representation on historical maps or a single, brief, archival mention. This applies to the *Manor Inn* at the east end of Thornton Rust village in Wensleydale. It was not named on any nineteenth-century OS map. Examination of the building's frontage teases out clues, though: at each end there was a granary, suggesting it had a brewhouse, and the frontage strongly suggests it was an inn, even though it was not on a major through route.

Coniston Inn, Coniston Cold

At the junction of the A65 and the Bell Busk road in Coniston Cold, west of Skipton, stands a house, with adjacent barn and outbuildings, once the *Coniston Inn* (SD904 550). In a trade directory for 1822 and in Quarter Sessions records for 1826 Peter Watson was listed as victualler, and it was still listed as an inn in 1837-38 trade directories, but not later ones, though 1840s OS maps did name it. It was ideally placed, fronting the pre-turnpike road and the Keighley-Kendal turnpike road created in 1753.

Granny House, Bell Busk

The shortest medieval road from Skipton to Settle led from Gargrave along Mark House Lane to Bell Busk, then via Otterburn, Hellifield Moor and Scaleber. Shortly before crossing the River Aire what is now Granville House was, possibly for centuries, *Granny House* (SD908 562). Whether it was a wayside inn or a hedge alehouse is unknown but in 1891 it was described merely as a 'public'. This old route was superseded in 1753 by the Keighley-Kendal turnpike road but one source believed the inn still served the public as late as 1820. [38] This is quite likely as packhorse men and drovers endeavoured to stick to old routes as they were often shorter – as this one – and were free of tolls.

Bay Horse Inn, Thorlby

The age-old highway and the turnpike road ran from Skipton through the hamlet of Thorlby along Sour Lane until the latter was re-routed in 1824. In the centre, at the road junction, is Bay Horse Farm which was the *Bay Horse Inn* (SD965 528). It was a coaching inn and the front garden was a cobbled yard; the long house frontage still has fixed iron rings where horses were tied up. In 1826 Joseph Atkinson was the licensee and in 1867 John Emmott was innholder. It did not appear on later OS maps.

4

Inns in Market Towns

Every market town had its complement of inns. Where the town was planned around a central square – or Market Place – they were arranged on all sides vying for regular and passing trade, as in Settle, Leyburn, Middleham and Richmond. Where the town was dominated by a High Street the inns were sited along both sides, again competing and trying to sell themselves as the most accessible and convenient places to stay, as in High Bentham, Sedbergh and Skipton.

Royal Oak, High Bentham

For several centuries the *Royal Oak* was one of High Bentham's premier inns, situated at the Main Street-Robin Lane junction, fronting what had been the King's Highway in medieval times. On the death of the owner, John Battersby, in 1835 it was put up for sale as 'All that Old Established and Well-accustomed INN or PUBLIC HOUSE' with brewhouse, stabling, shippon, barn, yard, croft etc. In 1904 and 1912, trade directories noted it just as a public house yet one from 1908 listed it as the Royal Oak Hotel 'with stabling and posting'.

Kings Arms, High Bentham

Before the middle of the nineteenth century the Royal Oak was eclipsed as High Bentham's main inn by the *Kings Arms*, also fronting the main road from Leeds to Lancaster, at the junction with what is now Station Road. From 1841-43, before the coming of the railway, this inn was a staging post for the mail coach from Leeds via Settle and Clapham to Lancaster. Recorded as an inn at least from 1650, it was refronted in 1741 by William Wilson, innholder. Its last licensee was Thomas Atkinson who sold it in 1866; the purchaser, Quaker John Rice, promptly gave up the licence.

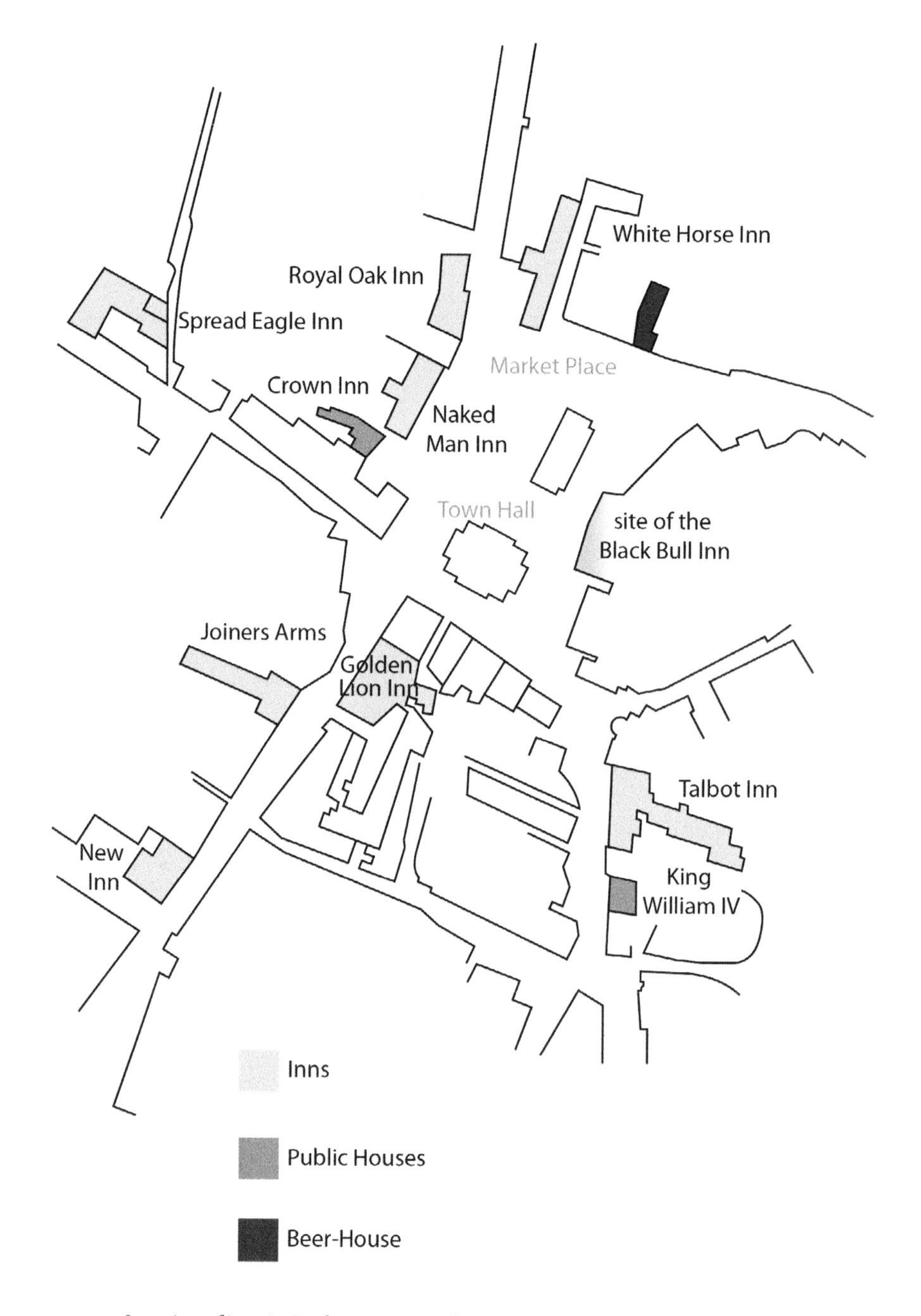

Location of inns in Settle town centre based on the tithe apportionment, 1844

Ten inns are known to have existed in Settle at one time or another (seven in 1822 and eight in 1840) and up to seven pubs and who knows how many beer-houses. Between 1789 and 1843 four stage coach services broke their journeys in Settle including the 'Diligence', the 'True Briton' and the 'Kendal Union'. In the early decades of the twentieth century Settle had four breweries: Bentleys behind the *Talbot Hotel*, Dutton's behind the *King William*, the Lion Brewery behind *Ashfield Hotel* and Massey's behind the *Golden Lion*. [39] In the nineteenth century twenty-two carriers were based in Settle, of which fifteen used an inn as their key staging post. In addition, until well into the twentieth century, Settle hosted regular livestock fairs and a produce market drawing in untold numbers of potential customers.

Naked Man

The will of John Cookeson of Settle, yeoman, dated 28 August 1690, itemised his possessions room by room: 'Red Chamber, Midle Chamber, Chamber over house, old Chambers, Kitching Loft, Low Parlor, higher Parlor, butterie, Cellar, Bodistead' and two barns. In all there were twenty-eight beds, five chamber pots, five tankards, eleven pans, umpteen pairs of sheets, blankets, coverlets, bolsters and thirty-four chairs and stools. Beyond any doubt this was an inn at that time. The date-stone bears the inscription 'JC 1663' ... and, by the way, has nothing to do with nakedness.

The will of Robert Cookson, also a Settle yeoman, dated 9 June 1702, listed 'Sun Chamber, Higher Chamber over the Parlor, Higher Chamber over the House, High Porch Chamber, Out Chamber over the Shopp, Parlor Chamber, Chamber over the house, Porch Chamber, Staire Case, bodystead, Parlor, Celler, Brewhouse, Stable, barne'. In the cellar were two large brewing pans, two large gelkers, three tearses, four barrels, and one hogs head. This was not just an inn: it was a substantial and busy inn.

In 1828 it was named along with sixteen other premises in Settle in the West Riding Quarter Sessions list of alehouse keepers. A legal document from 2 October 1832 referred to a dwellinghouse 'occupied as an Inn' called the Naked Man. The Settle Chronicle described it, on 1 March 1858, as 'the best adapted inn in the town, with a grocer's shop at the 'New End' – the section that is clearly newer than the original inn building.

Amongst other roles, the Naked Man acted as the staging post for carriers to Kendal (on Tuesdays, by J. Wrathall), to Bentham and Lancaster (Mondays and Thursdays, Thomas Charnley and Thomas Bentham), to Lancaster alone (Mondays and Thursdays, by Sedgwick's Waggons), to Austwick (Tuesdays, W. Lord), to Stainforth (Tuesdays and Saturdays, George Lund), and to Ingleton (also Tuesdays, James Foster).

As this late nineteenth-century photograph shows, it changed its identity from inn to hotel; it lost its licence in 1917. By 1929 it had become Ye Olde Naked Man café.

White Horse Inn

The former prominent Settle inn, the *White Horse*, is known from at least 1724 when the probate inventory of John Lawson, its owner, itemised 17 beds, 17 plates, 14 pewter dishes, 20 napkins and 24 blankets but only 3 (pewter) chamber pots, as well as 20 casks of ale each holding 100 gallons plus of ale in the cellar valued at £5 17s 6d. It was no mean inn. Rooms were named as 'Garrett, chamber over parlour, Sun Garrett, Garrett over the porch, porch chamber, Chamber over House, Chamber parlour, Chamber over shop, and house'[body]. There was a brewhouse, barn, garden and attached croft. An indenture from 1735 added to its list of appurtenances 'backsides', in other words a yard at the rear. In the 1740s it was run as an inn by Izat bell and Jane Hargraves, both widows; in 1806 by John Green. In 1888 a local almanac advertised that Henry Wilson, publican, offered 'well-aired beds ... good stabling ... and a horse and trap for hire'. It was also the stage terminus for carriers to destinations around Ingleborough on Tuesdays and Fridays. The White Horse was advertised as the White Horse Hotel in 1913, but as the White Horse PH in a 1928 trade directory.

Spread Eagle Inn

The *Spread Eagle Inn*, at one time simply the *Eagle* according to indentures from 1836, occupied most of the area either side of Spread Eagle Street where modern Kirkgate opens out above Victoria Hall. From 1807-43 it was the overnight stop for the Leeds-Kendal 'Kendal Union' stage coach, initially three days a week, latterly daily. The Hon. John Byng, who we have already met, stayed here in 1792 arriving on a 'dismal, black, raining day' and finding Settle a 'poor gloomy place'. William Bradley was the landlord and he cannot have been pleased with Byng's assessment of the inn: he spent his nights in a 'bad and dismal inn, with mice running about' in 'the worst inn's worst room'. When one considers what he had dined on he must be considered more than a little harsh in his judgement as he made no derogatory comments about the meals: his 'early dinner' consisting of beef steak, lamb chops, pickled salmon and tart set him back the princely sum of 9d; while his first night's supper was trout, lamb chops, potted trout and tart, again all for 9d. [40] From 1793-98 the Spread Eagle was listed in a directory as one of the town's two principal inns, with Bradley in charge. In 1794 there died Thomas Procter, sculptor and painter, whose father, Robert, had opened the Spread Eagle as an inn, after renovating an earlier structure, in 1734 running it as owner-innholder with his wife Ellen. Thomas, born here in 1753, suffered a miserable end in London.

In June 1850 the inn was put up for auction on the death of Robert Atkinson who owned or ran it, with its 'spacious yard' and stabling behind the inn, shippons, brewhouse, a coach house on the south side of the street, and a barn which is currently a garden shop. Settle's Tuesday markets and alternate Monday cattle fairs were given prominence as reasons to purchase the inn. The Spread Eagle ceased to be an inn in 1852.

Joiners Arms

Commercial Yard, off Duke Street in Settle, perpetuates the name of what in 1913 was the Commercial Hotel. The tall buildings that line Commercial Yard were stables, coach (or trap) house, ostlers' accommodation and part of what for more than a century was the *Joiners Arms*, yet another of the town's many inns. Various indentures and a mortgage, all from 1779, with William Willman, innholder, as one of the parties involved, concerned his 'new erected [house] now used as an Inn' called the Joiners Arms, complete with barn, two stables, brewhouse, a room over the brewhouse, warehouse, garden, orchard and the mandatory 'backside'.

Joiners Arms datestone

The 1774 datestone over the arch giving access to the yard from Duke Street confirms this 'new' build. He died in 1815, still the innholder, and William Tate took on the mantle after his death. The Joiners was the staging post for a weekly wagon service to Grassington via Airton and to Tosside, at least during the middle part of the nineteenth century; from 1816-43 for the 'True Briton' coach it was a calling point on its journeys three days a week between Kendal and Leeds. In 1857 Robert Atkinson was listed as 'victualler' here. The precise date when the Joiners became the Commercial has not been identified, but a trade directory for 1867 listed it as the Commercial Hotel and one for 1908 as the Commercial Temperance Hotel.

Joiners - courtyard

New Inn

At the corner of Station Road and Duke Street in Settle the rather unprepossessing building with an ornate doorway on the west side was the

New Inn. It is recorded as an inn from at least June 1814 when the innholder, E. Moorhouse, charged a customer 17s for dinner, drinks and horses' hay, which compared favourably with another bill, from March 1812, when the same cost £1 6s 4½d. According to the writer Howson, who we have met several times already, in 1850 this was one of Settle's two main inns, having knocked the Spread Eagle off its pedestal. As with other inns here, the New Inn was in partnership with carriers who connected Settle with Clitheroe on Thursdays and Colne on Saturdays in the early to mid nineteenth century, when it was owned by the wealthy Birkbeck family of tradesmen and landowners. It was still operational as a public house in 1904 but a trade directory for 1908 referred to it otherwise.

Settle's *Black Bull Inn* has long since been demolished and replaced by later buildings. It has rather a shadowy history and has not been found in trade directories and was not listed in the 1828 list of innholders. Its existence is, however, recorded in legal indentures: in 1751, 1753 and 1755, for example, Thomas Capstacke was the innholder, though not the owner, and the premises included stables, brewhouse and other outbuildings so it was definitely an inn rather than just a public house. A later indenture, from 1826, is telling: the document clearly states '... formerly used as an Inn and called and known by the name of the Black Bull ...' Exactly when it went out of business is not known but it cannot have been much before 1826.

Bell Inn, Giggleswick

The *Bell Inn*, at the top of Belle Hill in Giggleswick, is recorded from as long ago as a 1579 Clifford estate survey, though not necessarily as an inn – an alehouse perhaps. It has been said that the inn was named after the steep road down into the village centre – Belle Hill – but it is more likely to have been the other way round. Historically, bell and belle were interchangeable and it was common for alehouses to announce the availability of a fresh brew by tolling a bell. Two deeds from 1717 concerned the transfer of ownership of the Bell Inn and other properties within the Claphamson family but, three years later, father and son sold it on to William Wiglesworth of Woodfield near Ribchester. The 1717 deeds specifically called it the 'Bell Inn' whereas the 1720 deed simply said 'commonly called Bell' with no hint that it was still an inn. If this did mark its end as a hostelry, it missed out on the potential trade when the turnpike road re-routed the ancient east-west highway past its door.

At the bottom of Belle Hill stood the *Old Harts Head Inn*. It lay on the historical route, and the first turnpike road (from 1753) that took travellers through Settle down Spread Eagle Street to cross the Ribble at Kendalman's Ford, then past the foot of Belle Hill and Giggleswick parish church to ascend the steep hill along Craven Bank Lane. It may have an origin as an inn from the seventeenth century; an indenture from 1787 described its having a brewhouse, barns, stables and malt kiln at the rear, occupied by Jane Bradley as innholder. A deed from 1804 related to a property 'next above a certain Inn called the Hart head' but a further deed, from 1806, called it *Hart Head* without mentioning either inn or brewhouse. This is because the turnpike road had been re-routed in 1804 to cross Settle Bridge and avoid Giggleswick: it now ran up Buck Haw Brow and the owner of the old Harts Head, Robert Garstang, looked into his crystal ball, saw the future, and built the new Harts Head fronting the new road. (See page 15)

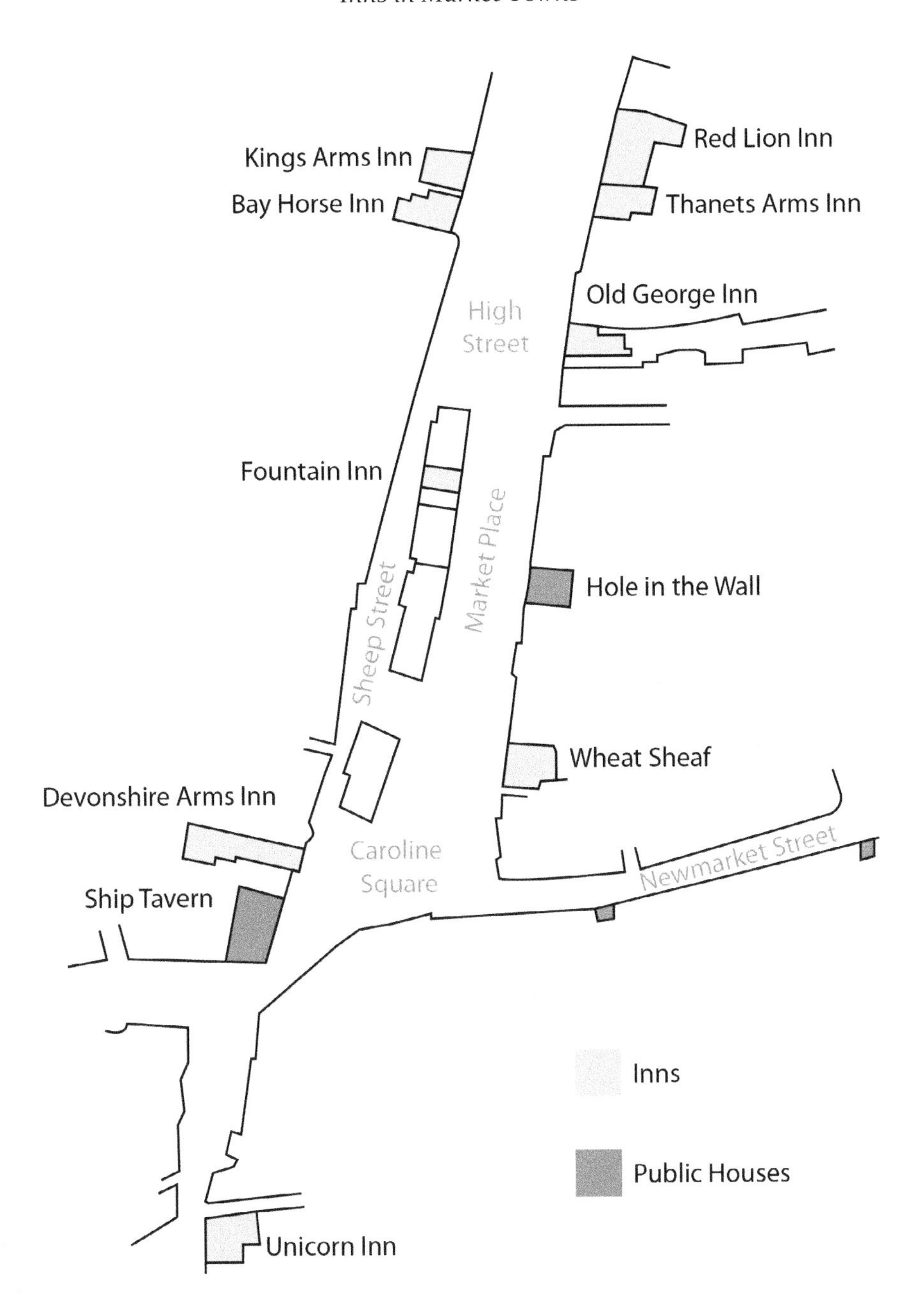

Location of inns in Skipton town centre based on a mid-19th-century OS map

In the nineteenth century Skipton's High Street, and its former southern extension called Market Place, had ten inns though there were others away from the town centre. In 1822 the town as a whole had nineteen licensed houses, in 1840 twenty-four with a further eleven beer-houses. By 1907 OS maps showed five of these as public houses and one as a hotel while one had disappeared: this reflects the town's changing economy. From at least 1597 to 1906, Skipton's town-centre cattle fairs were a significant contributor to its prosperity, and census records for 1841-91 show that ten inns were favoured by drovers and cattle dealers. In June 1841 (on census night) twenty-six drovers and dealers stayed overnight, in 1851 fifteen, 1861 only one, 1871 thirty-five, 1881 none, 1891 twenty-one and 1901 three. The most favoured inns were the *Old George* (twenty-seven in total), the *Royal Oak* (twenty-three) and the *King's Arms* and the *Hole in the Wall* nine each: in all 110 drovers or cattle dealers were recorded on census nights.

Three of the inns were noted as Skipton's premier inns in coaching days: the *Black Horse* at the top of High Street, the *Devonshire Arms* in Caroline Square and, from 1790, the *New Inn* on Newmarket Street (from 1810 called the *Devonshire Hotel* and now Wetherspoons). Byng used the Black Horse for his stay in Skipton and it will come as no surprise to hear that he was less than complimentary, disparaging both service and facilities.

Kings Arms
(Photograph reproduced by kind permission of the Ellwood family, Mrs V. Rowley, and North Yorkshire County Council, Skipton Library, www.rowleycollection.co.uk)

The *Kings Arms* was one of Skipton's oldest inns being recorded in a Clifford estate survey in 1605. It was much frequented by cattle dealers and drovers but, by 1861, had transformed itself from inn to hotel and, by 1871, was in the hands of Henry Manby, 'Ironmonger and Publican'. It closed in 1967 and was demolished soon after. This photograph was taken between 1964 and 1967.

Bay Horse

Also a coaching inn and favoured by drovers, the *Bay Horse Inn* was demolished as early as 1898, a graphic illustration of how Skipton's trade-based prosperity was declining. It is commemorated now by this sign over an arch giving access to the inn's former yard.

Royal Oak

Located at the corner of Water Street and Mill Bridge, the *Royal Oak Inn* was one of the most popular inns among cattle dealers and drovers. It is one of the latest Skipton hostelries to succumb to changing trends in drinking having closed down in 2010.

Old George
(Photograph reproduced by kind permission of the Ellwood family, Mrs V. Rowley, and North Yorkshire County Council, Skipton Library, www.rowleycollection.co.uk)

At least as old as the Kings Arms, the *George Inn* was rebadged as the *Old George* in 1807, and was among Skipton's most impressive inns despite not having achieved the status of a top-tier inn. In 1890 the then owner added the third floor to make it fit in with buildings on either side. It closed in 1971 and was converted to high-class retail use but the exterior of the two upper floors is still recognisable today. This inn was first choice for many cattle dealers and drovers and did not necessarily insist on 'quality' customers. On census night, 1891, a 60-year-old Irish drover known as 'Black Jack' kept himself apart from six other Irish drovers by settling for a doss 'with the cattle in the barn'. The 1901 census recorded in residence, amongst others, an ostler, two maids, a kitchen maid and a 'boots'; Black Jack would have had no use for any of them. This photograph was taken after 1970.

White Swan, Middleham

Once a busy market town, a staging post in the 1830s for the 'Highflyer' mail coach at the end of a gruelling seven-hour journey from Leeds, the focus of a major cattle fair on Middleham Moor until eclipsed by Leyburn, and long renowned for its concentration on racehorse training, Middleham had more than its fair share of inns. In the 1820s five premises were licensed, in 1840 eight, in 1890 six, and there are still several traditional inns ranged around Market Place. Inevitably perhaps, John Byng broke his travels here in June 1792 staying two nights at the *White Swan Inn*, now the Wensleydale Hotel. His diary records that as he approached the town centre he thought it a 'sorry inn' but, for once, he was not scathing about either food or accommodation. He was shown into a 'clean parlour' where he ordered 'several trout' for his dinner – several! However, he made sure to give the cook precise instructions on how he wanted them cooked and served. Presumably on his second night, he feasted on 'A Boiled Fowl, Cold Ham, Yorkshire Pudding, Loyn of Mutton Roast, Gooseberry Pie, Cheesecakes ... A better dinner and better dress'd I never sat down to', he opined. His bill for two nights food and board, wine, brandy and horse's corn came to the princely sum of £1 0s 11d, with his gargantuan dinner accounting for 1s 3d of this.

White Boar, Middleham

On the approach to Market Place from Middleham Bridge the *White Boar Inn* was the first to be encountered: its former role is perpetuated with the sign hanging outside. It was not mentioned in the 1822 or 1828 licensing lists, or in trade directories from 1823, 1840 or 1890: perhaps it had changed its name.

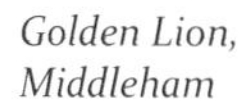

Golden Lion, Middleham

On the south side of Market Place the *Golden Lion Inn* was also not mentioned in the directories. It bears a datestone 'K 1682 HA' but its life story is not fully known. Its first appearance in trade directories was in 1890 when Mrs D. Dinsdale was licensee, and it was also entered in a 1908 directory.

Blue Bell, Richmond

In 1579 Richmond had no less than twenty-four inns and taverns; in 1686 the town offered overnight stabling for 228 horses and beds for ninety-nine travellers; in 1756 these numbers had grown to c. 1000 and 521 respectively. [41] In 1823 there were twenty-two licensed houses, and in 1890 eighteen. Market Place still has more than enough inns and pubs to allow determined drinkers to imbibe in a different one every night of the week. The *Blue Bell Inn* was one of Richmond's inns but, after closing down, was less than tastefully re-fronted on the ground floor when it became a Woolworth's store in 1979. The upper floors, however, retain the external glory that was this inn.

Kings Arms, Richmond

Recorded from at least 1679 when it was owned by Henry Sober (and what a name for a publican to have), the *Kings Arms Inn* was also very prominent on the north side of Market Place but when King Street was created more than half of the inn was demolished with the narrow white building on the left side of the street being all that remains. However, S. Metcalfe was noted as occupier in 1820. [42]

Commercial Inn, Leyburn

Leyburn eclipsed Middleham as the main market town for lower Wensleydale after its charter was granted in 1686 and, like all such towns, a series of inns grew up around Market Place with, for example, three inns, five public houses and several beer-houses licensed in the 1820s. Among them, at the corner of Market Place and Wensley Road, was an inn named on an 1808 estate map as the *Commercial Inn*, though it did not appear on the 1820s list of licensed premises.

White Hart Inn, Sedbergh

As with all market towns Sedbergh had a broad range of inns and public houses – at least sixteen, of which five definitely had 'inn' in their name. At the corner of Main Street and Finkle Street stood the *Bull and Dog Inn* which is recorded from before 1740; by 1837 it was known as the *White Hart Inn*. The building seen today – now used as a Sports and Social Club – had morphed into the *White Hart Hotel* by 1873 and was substantially rebuilt after being bought by a Kendal brewery in 1899. [43] Its life as an inn or pub came to an end in the 1970s.

Chapter 5

Pubs – the Archetypal 'Local'

There cannot be a village anywhere that did not have at least one pub which, as we saw earlier, was often in competition with the church for 'customers', and concerning which some clergyman found themselves personally conflicted. This chapter presents a selection of locals from across the Yorkshire Dales, as far as possible putting them in their local context.

Moon's Acre, High Bentham

On the western edge of High Bentham is a house long called Moon's Acre. In the 1820s John Titterington built a brewery, malt kiln and what was probably a beer-house on the site, and 'Moonsacre' was named on the tithe apportionment map. There is no record of what his beer-house was called but barely visible on the front door lintel is the painted sign 'JOHN TITTERINGTON LICENSED DEALER IN ...'. His son, William, inherited the business but bankruptcy brought it all to an end.

Potters/Joiners Arms, Burton in Lonsdale

The scale of Burton in Lonsdale's industrial economy almost inevitably led to the growth of a plethora of public houses. Indeed, it is known to have had at least eight licensed houses. At the top of Duke Street the *Potters Arms* reflected the nature of the village's main industry. A Sales Notice from 1852 announced that various properties were to be sold at Richard Bateson's *The Potters Arms Inn* though it was most likely more of a pub than a true inn. At some point its name changed to the *Joiners Arms*; it closed down in 1988.

Black Bull, Burton in Lonsdale

This may well have been an inn originally, facing the main road through Burton in Lonsdale village. A trade directory from 1822 called it the *Old Black Bull* and in 1895 it was described as a farmhouse 'formerly the Black Bull Inn'.

New Inn, Burton in Lonsdale

On the corner of High Street and Duke Street in Burton in Lonsdale was the *New Inn*. Its first record seems to be a deed from 1843 but it does not appear in later directories so may have been short lived. [44]

Plough Inn, High Bentham

High Bentham was an important market town with a range of licensed premises, including the *Plough Inn* in the centre of the village. It is surely too small to have been a true inn, and it has little written history other than that it was listed in a trade directory in 1867 and is known to have shut down in 1914, victim of wartime screw tightening.

New Inn, Westhouse (Author's Collection)

Equally shadowy is another very local 'local', the long-since demolished *New Inn* at Westhouse, west of Ingleton. This image was taken in the early nineteenth century.

Cross Keys, Ingleton

Like so many locals, there is little to say of the *Cross Keys*, tucked away in the centre of Ingleton.

Spindle Tree, Clapham

On the east side of Clapham Beck, at Gildersbank, the *Spindle Tree* was one of several premises that came to life during the Clapham's periodic livestock fairs.

King William, Giggleswick

This public house has not been located in any nineteenth-century trade directory or early map, apart from an 1857 directory, and its date of demise has also not been determined.

Board/Crown, Settle

In 1835, according to an indenture, *The Board* was occupied by John Holroyd though the text focussed on a 'Dwellinghouse Dramhouse liquor cellary and vaults' which had hitherto 'formerly [been] occupied as a public house and Dramshop' called the Board. From details within the indenture, this can only have been what later was called the *Crown Inn*, listed as such in a trade directory of 1867 and an indenture of 1879 by which 'Henry Holden of Settle, spirit merchant' sold to Edmund Crabtree the 'inn called the Crown Inn'. By an advertisement in 1887 Robert Batty offered potential customers 'good stabling' and a Sales Notice of 1891 announced the impending auction of 'The Crown Hotel' – had Batty fallen on hard times? This was not its end, though, as in 1909 it was operating as a carrier station. It shut down either in 1914 or 1917.

SETTLE.

MR. CHARLES E. TOWLER

WILL

OFFER FOR SALE BY AUCTION,

AT THE

CROWN HOTEL, SETTLE,

On Tuesday, the 19th May, 1891,

At 2.30 p.m., precisely and subject to Conditions of Sale,

THE FULLY LICENSED PUBLIC HOUSE,

KNOWN AS

The "Crown Hotel," Settle,

COMPRISING:

Bar, Bar Parlour, Front Parlour, Smoke Room, Two Large Kitchens, Four Good Cellars, Upstairs Sitting-Room, Three Bedrooms, Large Room over Kitchen, Bath Room, W.C., and Large Attic, as now in the occupation of Mr. Robert Batty.

The Property is leasehold for a long term of years, and subject to the payment of a yearly ground rent of 4/6.

The Hotel faces the Market Place, in Settle, and, being well tenanted and much frequented by excursionists, affords a favourable investment to Brewers and Capitalists.

For further information apply to

WRIGHT, CHARLESWORTH & Co.,

SOLICITORS,

SETTLE AND SKIPTON.

Sales Notice for The Crown Hotel public house, Settle, 1891

Bay Horse, Langcliffe

Christopher Wright ran a beer-house at Westview in Langcliffe, called the *Bay Horse*, and on one night in 1871 two men working on building the Settle-Carlisle railway got themselves into such a state that they refused to leave at closing time and set about Wright to the extent that he died of his injuries several days later. Five years' penal servitude was handed out and the beer-house lost its licence, though local anecdote says it continued long afterwards without a licence. [45]

Golden Lion, Selside

Even a settlement as tiny as Selside in Upper Ribblesdale had its local. Thomas or Marmaduke Greenbank was innkeeper here in 1798 in what was named on 1851 OS mapping as the *Golden Lion*. In 1807 the burial of Anthony Egglin of Selside, innkeeper, was entered in the parish register. It stopped serving c. 1963.

Old Cross Keys, Rathmell

OS mapping from 1848 and 1892 both named the '*Old Cross Keys PH*' at the northern end of Rathmell, south of Settle. It was also listed in the 'Craven Almanac' in 1928 but had fewer than ten more years or so of licensed life.

Red Lion, Gargrave

At the far western end of Gargrave, fronting High Street, is a row of cottages part of which was the *Red Lion* PH. In 1822 and 1826 Henry Ward was licensee and it was named on 1840s OS maps but not on later maps or in trade directories. It is yet another local presumably taken for granted.

Grouse Tavern, Gargrave

On the corner of West Street and High Street, Gargrave, what ended up as the Grouse Hotel started life as *The Grouse Tavern*, later the *Grouse PH*. It appeared on OS mapping from the late 1840s and closed down around 1970. It is now houses still called The Grouse.

Wonder Inn, Dent

A short distance below Denthead, what is now Scow Cottage, or an earlier building, was one of several temporary public houses cum boarding houses for navvies working on building the Settle-Carlisle Railway, this one known as the *Wonder Inn*.

White Hart, Dent

White Hart House, close to the Adam Sedgwick Memorial in Dent, was the *White Hart* public house, recorded in a directory in 1838 but closed between 1891 and 1901. The pub was the section with the For Sale sign.

Swettenham Arms, Sedbergh

One of Sedbergh's public houses, on Back Lane, was the *Swettenham Arms*, of which little is known.

Black Horse, Killington

Set at a cross-roads 3 km west of Sedbergh, the former *Black Horse* public house (SD620 917) still carries the black-horse crest on its frontage. It belonged to the Upton family who owned nearby Ingmire Hall Estate from 1577-1903, and a black horse was one element of their family coat of arms. It was for many years colloquially known as *Scotch Jeans* suggesting a link with the long-lasting north-south drove trade. It was listed as a public house on the 1858 OS map but not in 1896.

The Windmill, Kettlewell

On Far Lane, Kettlewell, part of this row of houses was a public house called *The Windmill*, recorded only in a trade directory from 1837, and shown on an

OS map from 1847-48 as a public house, but not on later maps. Presumably it was short- lived.

Catch-all Inn, Swinden photographed not long before it was shut down. (Courtesy Ben McKenzie)

Opposite the entrance to Swinden Quarry, south of Grassington, stands a rather gaunt three-storey house with a rather chequered history (SD986 618). In 1845 proposals were put forward to construct a railway from Grassington via Kettlewell tunnelling under the fells to emerge in Bishopdale, but they failed. Further proposals were submitted in 1865. Thinking that he saw an opportunity ahead the owner opened this building as the *Railway Tavern* (1867 trade directory), otherwise referred to as *Swinden End* (OS map from 1853). It seemed a sound plan at the time, but the railway was never built despite several other attempts to secure financial and political backing. However, it carried on rebranded as the *Catch-all Inn* (OS map 1891). In 1902 P.W. Spencer & Co. took on the lease of Swinden Quarry, using the line which was constructed as far as Threshfield by that year. Six years later the company bought the pub and promptly shut it down: apparently, quarrymen were wont to pop across the road in their lunch break to quench their copious thirst. Whether the Spencers had health and safety uppermost in their mind or felt the afternoon shift's quality control was adversely affected by too much ale is a moot point.

The Jobbers Inn/Commercial Inn, Grassington

At the foot of Main Street in Grassington, and currently a bank, this building was called *The Jobbers Inn* (or *Arms*) on the 1852 OS map and in a trade directory from 1867, but it was not recorded in the 1820s licensing lists so cannot have been an inn – more likely a pub anyway – at that time. Later on its name changed to the *Commercial Inn*. This image dates from c. 1900.

The Blue Anchor, Grassington

A settlement as busy as Grassington was bound to have had numerous pubs and beer-houses; Main Street had its full complement, among which was the curiously-named *Blue Anchor*, still painted blue and with part of it perpetuating the name. Like several of the town's public houses, its recorded history is scant.

Masons Arms, Eastby

Recorded since at least the 1820s, this 'local' is one of the most recent to have called 'last orders' for the last time, unable to withstand modern economic and social forces. Despite local protestations about ripping the heart out of Eastby, the *Masons Arms*, on Barden Road in the village, was closed down in 2011 by the pub chain that owned it. It is now a dwelling.

The New Ship, Skipton

The *New Ship* on Mill Bridge in Skipton is first recorded in 1799 and remained open until 1974 though it almost lost its licence, as did so many of Skipton's pubs, when the cattle fairs were removed from High Street to a more suitable site in 1906. It must stand out in the sense that successive generations of the

Alderson family ran it from 1844 to 1942: maybe that is why it had survived attempts to deprive it of its licence. *(Photograph reproduced by kind permission of the Ellwood family, Mrs V. Rowley, and North Yorkshire County Council, Skipton Library, www.rowleycollection.co.uk)*

Wheat Sheaf, Skipton

The *Wheat Sheaf* public house is recorded from 1754 when it was most likely an alehouse, sited in Caroline Square at the bottom of High Street. As this image suggests, in its latter days it was a stereotypical 'local'. From 1892-96 and 1901-03 Squire Firth was mine host; it fell foul of the authorities' desire to clean up the town after the cattle fairs were moved, and closed in 1906. *(Photograph reproduced by kind permission of the Ellwood family, Mrs V. Rowley, and North Yorkshire County Council, Skipton Library, www.rowleycollection.co.uk)*

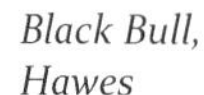

Black Bull, Hawes

The choice of inns and pubs in Hawes was increased by one when the *Black Bull* opened its doors on the north side of Market Place. The list of licensed premises for 1822-23 includes one called *The Bull* whereas that for 1828-29 has the *Black Bull*: whether they were one and the same is not known though two were called 'Bull' in the former list. Late nineteenth-century maps mark it as 'Inn', unnamed. It closed down in 1959 and has gone through several guises since then as café or guest house.

Sun Inn, Gayle

The settlement of Gayle, south of Hawes, hardly seems large enough to have had a pub but it did – the *Sun Inn*, now Bridge End Cottage. Not much can be said about it other than it had closed down by 1891.

Shoulder of Mutton, Burtersett

Dominating the row of houses called Middlegate in Burtersett, Wensleydale, was the *Shoulder of Mutton*, now Hillcrest House. It served the needs of

Burtersett's flagstone quarrymen but rather relied on their custom to remain viable. From 1795-1825 William Kilburn was in occupation and it had shut down by 1850 at the latest even though the stone mines were worked for another eighty or so years.

Queens Arms, Askrigg

Askrigg was a far busier place than Burtersett and was able to support at least five licensed premises, one of which was the *Queens Arms* towards the upper end of Main Street. The name is preserved in the modern house called Queen's Lea though the public house also encompassed Seata House next door. It was not listed in Quarter Sessions records unless it operated then under another name.

Miners Arms, Woodhall

Between Askrigg and Castle Bolton in Wensleydale, lead mining employed variable numbers of men and the *Miners Arms* public house at Woodhall (SD977 903) catered for the needs of those who toiled in Woodhall Mine. The mine has a recorded history from 1664-1886; the pub was listed in Quarter Sessions records in the 1820s, in 1834 when Jonathan Knowles was the licensee, and in 1854. It was not marked on the 1891 OS map.

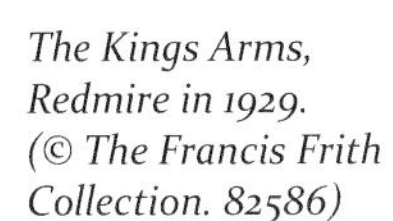

The Kings Arms, Redmire in 1929. (© The Francis Frith Collection. 82586)

Tucked down a back street in Redmire, the *Kings Arms* was a true village 'local'. It is recorded from at least 1822 and this image was taken in 1929. Its date of closure has not been found.

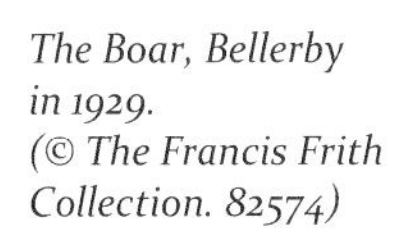

The Boar, Bellerby in 1929. (© The Francis Frith Collection. 82574)

In Quarter Sessions records for 1828-29 there were two licensed premises in Bellerby, north of Leyburn: *The Board* and *The Pig*. The 1854 OS map marked *The Boar PH* at the north end of the village. It is possible that they were one and the same, that the letter 'd' in the original name 'Board' was dropped to avoid associations with beer-house origins. The 1891 OS map simply marked 'Inn', not that it ever was an inn. This photograph was taken in 1929 when it was *The Boar*.

The Loyal Dales Volunteer, Thoralby

Facing south to overlook The Green in Thoralby, Wensleydale, was a public house called the *Loyal Dales Volunteer*. The building bears a datestone 'J & RW 1811' which is broadly contemporary with this pub's inception. When the renewed threat of invasion by Napoleon's troops raised its ugly head nineteen regiments of volunteers were formed across the North Riding: one of them was raised under Col. M.T. Straubenzee in 1805 and was called the Loyal Dales Volunteers. The regiment's flag still hangs in Wensley Church. To name a pub after a regiment was seen as a patriotic gesture. When Boney was finally defeated in 1815 the regiments were disbanded. The pub was recorded in Quarter Sessions records in the 1820s, on the 1857 OS map and in a trade directory in 1890 as the *Volunteer* but it was not named on OS maps from 1891.

The Viscount/Topham Arms, Melmerby

In 1823 a trade directory named two pubs in Melmerby: the *Bay Horse* and the *Board*; another directory, from 1840, named *The Viscount*, as did the 1857 OS map. A directory from 1890 had the same premises as the *Topham Arms*, renamed after one of Coverdale's historical landowning families. The OS map a year later just marked 'PH' while the 1910 edition from 1910 named *Topham Arms PH*. The building today preserves its licensed past as Topham Arms House.

Shoulder of Mutton, Reeth

Overlooking The Green in Reeth, Swaledale, on the western side there were four inns and public houses all serving the town's market functions as well as mining communities from round about. Two are still operational. Towards the top of the row was the *Shoulder of Mutton* public house. It was listed in a trade directory from 1823 and shown on the 1857 OS map but not on later editions. A later directory, from 1889, did list it but a year later it was unoccupied. Its licence was revoked in 1892.

Half Moon, Reeth

The last building at the lower end of the row was also a public house, *The Half Moon*, now Half Moon Cottage. It was recorded on the 1857 OS map, listed in a trade directory for 1890 and still open into the new century with Mary Close as licensee. The OS map from 1910-11 named it as a public house but the 1911 census did not give Mary's occupation as innkeeper or victualler. Presumably, it closed down around that date.

The Miners Arms, Low Row

Opposite the Methodist Chapel in Low Row, Swaledale, stands an impressive house that was once a public house. Few dates or documentary references have been found for it other than its inclusion on the 1854 OS map and census records. There is a possible clue on the lintel stone above the front door: clearly visible is the painted name 'William Lowe': the nature of the sign is typical of licensed premises. This pub may have started life in the 1820s as yet another *Board*, may have become the *Miners Arms* by 1840 and the *Queens Arms* in 1879. William Lowe, lead miner, was recorded on the 1871 census in occupation of the *Temperance Hotel* in Low Row so it must have had an interlude between being the *Miners* and the *Queens*. By 1881 Edmund Coates was in charge of the *Queens*, and was still there in 1891 and by the 1901 census occupied licensed premises in Low Row called the *Tavern* but by 1911 was employed as huntsman for the Swaledale Hunt. Backtracking a little, he occupied the *Commercial Inn* in Low Row in 1871 and an unnamed inn in 1861. The small house adjacent and attached to what had been the *Miners/Queens* is now called Billy Gill's Cottage: in 1891 William Gill – grocer, draper and farmer – occupied the *Temperance Hotel*. Thus, in 1891, both the *Queens* and the *Temperance Hotel* must have coexisted side by side. By 1911 the Queens/Tavern had lost its licence. It is all rather confusing.

Black Bull, Langthwaite

Arkengarthdale was equally involved in lead mining and every community had its pubs. Tiny Langthwaite had two including the *Black Bull* public house, set well back behind the former Primitive Methodist Chapel. In 1840 John Wray was the occupier of the 'Bull'; it was not listed in later directories though it was named as the Black Bull on OS maps from the 1850s

Rose and Crown, Whaw

Even smaller than Langthwaite is Whaw, 3 km further up the dale, yet again in lead-mining country. The building shown in the centre of this view was the *Rose and Crown* public house, shown as such on 1850s OS maps; its name changed from *Board* to *Rose and Crown* in 1854. It was not named in later trade directories and it could not have survived once mining started its terminal decline.

Crown Vaults, Leyburn

The Bolton Hall estate map of 1808, mentioned earlier, marked and named three public houses in the centre of Leyburn. The *Crown Vaults* stood at the corner of High Street and Harmby Road, behind the Town Hall. It was listed as just the *Crown* in 1830 and 1890. Its date of closure has not been identified.

Wheat Sheaf, Leyburn

Where Market Place in Leyburn becomes Railway Street the *Wheat Sheaf* public house occupied a prime position and may originally have served as an inn. It was also depicted on the 1808 map but has not been found in documentary sources.

Pig and Whistle/Oddfellows Arms, Leyburn

Next door to the *Commercial Inn* in Leyburn stands a building that was named as the *Pig and Whistle* on the 1808 map but the *Oddfellows Arms* from 1840 to the 1870s; it was not included on the 1891 OS map which, in fact, is not helpful here as only the *Bolton Arms* was deemed worthy of naming.

Sources and Notes

Sources

Many of the buildings included in this book have been found by many years of searching through likely sources of secondary information, such as local guides and historical books, historical mapping, contemporary trade directories and newspapers. Much useful information is available in the Quarter Sessions records for the North Riding and West Riding, held respectively at the North Yorkshire County Record Office (NYCRO), Northallerton, and the Wakefield History Centre (WRRD, WHC); these list all licensed innkeepers by place and year, but only by hostelry in the 1820s. Indentures of Sale or Lease provide very detailed information and usually name the inn or beer-house. Those for the North Riding are held at the North Riding Registry of Deeds, NYCRO, Northallerton, and for the West Riding at the WRRD, WHC, Wakefield. Wills and inventories are located at The Borthwick Institute for Archives at the University of York: transcriptions of Craven wills and inventories can be accessed at www.dalescommunityarchives.org.uk. For North Craven *Lambert's Settle Almanac* is invaluable, listing by township names of innkeepers and inns for the late nineteenth and early twentieth centuries. Similarly, various runs of trade directories for the North and West Ridings provide useful data, especially Kelly's, White's, Baines' and Post Office Directories. Historical mapping can be a useful source for identifying the precise location of rural hostelries, especially Ordnance Survey (OS) six-inch mapping and turnpike trust route maps. Census returns are invaluable from 1851-1911. Readers may also find of use the sources listed under Further Reading.

Notes

See the Further Reading section for detailed references.

1. Speight, 1897, 68.
2. Earle, J. 1811. *Microcosmography; Or, a Piece of the World Discovered: In Essays and Characters.* London: John Harding; and Whitehead and Cochrane, p. 38.
3. Mass-Observation. 1987. *The Pub and the People. A Worktown study.* London: The Cresset Library, p. 41.
4. Blackmore, R.D. 1869. *Lorna Doone.* London: Collins (1952 ed.), p. 405.
5. www.english-heritage.org/publications/iha-ships-boats/late. Accessed 29 June 2012.

6. Cumbria Archive Service, Kendal. WDRY. Fleming Archive.
7. Townend, M. 2014. *Viking Age Yorkshire*. Pickering: Blackthorn Press.
8. Salzman, L. F. 1923. *English Industries of the Middle Ages*. Oxford: Clarendon Press, pp. 285-94.
9. Legg, K.J. 2009. *The Lost Cartulary of Bolton Priory*. YAS Record Series 160. Woodbridge: Boydell Press, p. 114, f.222.
10. Statutes of the Realm IV (1), 4 Edw VI.C.3, p. 102; Brander 1973, p. 41.
11. Craig, W. J. 1984 and 1985. 'James Ryther of Harewood and his letters to William Cecil, Lord Burghley' *Yorkshire Archaeological Journal* part 1, 56, pp. 95-118; part 2 57, pp. 125-47.
12. Speight 1897, 130.
13. Bimson, M. 1970. 'The significance of "Ale-Measure" Marks' Post-Medieval Archaeology 4, pp. 165-66 (on the Act for Ascertaining the Measures for Retailing Ale and Beer 1700, from which Act this tankard resulted).
14. Gilchrist, R. 2018. *Medieval Life. Archaeology and the Life Course.* Woodbridge: Boydell Press.
15. Speight 1897, 240, 493.
16. I have never been able to erase from my memory bank one experience many years ago in my African days when driving alone through mostly empty 'bush' for a whole day. I arrived at a mission station in the late afternoon to spend the night and was made welcome by the two resident Brothers, like me in their mid twenties, who soon produced a bottle of rather nice whisky from a well-hidden nook. About an hour later there was hilarious and manic panic as they removed all evidence of our 'misdemeanour' – the Father's Landrover was heard approaching and to him alcohol was the personification of evil. The evening meal was an absolute masterclass in trying to keep three straight faces.
17. Hoskin, P, Sandall, S. and Watson, E . 2011. 'The court records of the Diocese of York 1300 – 1858: An under-used resource' *Yorkshire Archaeological Journal* 83, pp. 148-63.
18. Smail, J. (ed.) 2001. *Woollen Manufacturing in Yorkshire. The Memorandum Books of John Brearley, Cloth Frizzer at Wakefield 1758-1762.* YAS Record Series 65. Woodbridge: The Boydell Press.
19. Napey, nappy or noppy were slang terms for very strong ale.
20. The Borthwick Institute for Archives, vol. 73, f.16; vol. 83, f. 9; vol. 87, f. 8.
21. NYCRO. QDL (V). Records of Victuallers and Alehouse Keepers: North Riding Quarter Sessions. For the West Riding see WRRD. QE32. Alehouses and Licensed Premises. Recognisances.
22. Mass-Observation 1987, passim.
23. Hatcher 1990, 43.

24. Riley n.d., 28.
25. Riley n.d., 26.
26. Crowther 1930, 114.
27. Hartley and Ingilby 1963, 38.
28. Hurtley 1786, 32.
29. Housman 1814, 25.
30. Howson 1850, 33.
31. Speight 1897, 375.
32. West Yorkshire Archive Service, Morley. WYL 524/325.
33. Bruyn Andrews 1970, 53, 88-89.
34. NYCRO. ZTW III 2/168, letter J. Hammond, West Burton to George Dudgeon, Settle.
35. Butterworth 1993, 40.
36. Joynes 2006, 284.
37. Speight 1897, 323.
38. Gray 1891, 263.
39. NYCRO. ZXF(M), 1/7/30, n.d.
40. Bruyn Andrews 1970, 94-96.
41. Fieldhouse and Jennings 1978, 171-72.
42. Clarkson 1821, Appendix, lix.
43. Lancaster 1986; Scobie 2010.
44. Stan Lawrence Archive, Lancaster University Library, Special Collections. SLA 2/3, Misc. Record Cards – BL.
45. Langcliffe 2000, 48-52.

Further Reading

The reader who wishes to delve deeper into the rich history of hostelries will find the following titles useful.

Addison, Sir W. 1980. *The Old Roads of England*. London: Batsford. (Contains a chapter on coaching inns)

Bennett, J.M. 1986. 'The village ale-wife: women and brewing in 14th-century England' in B.A. Hanawalt (ed.). *Women and Work in Preindustrial Europe*. Bloomington: Indiana University Press, pp. 20-36.

Bennett, J. M. 1996. *Ale, Beer and Brewsters in England: Women's Work in a Changing World*, 1300 to 1600. Oxford: Oxford University Press.

Bonser, K.J. 1970. *The Drovers*. London: Macmillan.

Bradley, T. 1889. *The Old Coaching Days in Yorkshire*. Leeds: Yorkshire Conservative Newspaper Co. ("The Yorkshire Post").

Brander, M. 1973. *The Life and Sport of the Inn*. London: Gentry Books.

Brandwood, G, Davison, A. and Slaughter, M. 2004. *Licensed to Sell. The History and Heritage of the Public House*. London: English Heritage. (Very comprehensive).

Brown, P. 2010. *Man Walks into a Pub. A Sociable History of Beer*. London: Pan Books. (A light-hearted national history of pubs and pubbing).

Bruyn Andrews, C. (ed.). 1970. *The Torrington Diaries*, vol. 3. (first published 1936). New York: Barnes and Noble; London: Methuen.

Burke, T. 1927. *The Book of the Inn*. London: Constable.

Butterworth, K. and A. 1993. 'Once in Preston under Scar'. *The Story of a Wensleydale Village*. Privately published.

Clark, P. 1983. *The English Alehouse. A Social History 1200 – 1830*. London: Longman.

Clarkson, C. 1821. *The History and Antiquities of Richmond in the County of York*. Richmond: C. Clarkson.

Crowther, J. 1930. *"Silva Gars" (Grass Wood) Grassington*. Keighley: The Rydal Press.

Fieldhouse, R. and Jennings, B. 1978. *A History of Richmond and Swaledale*. London and Chichester: Phillimore.

'Gray, Johnnie'. 1891. *Through Airedale from Goole to Malham*. Leeds: Walker & Laycock. (Johnnie Gray was the nom de plume of Harry Speight).

Hartley, M. and Ingilby, J. 1963. *The Yorkshire Dales.* London: J.M. Dent.

Hatcher, J. 1990. *Richmondshire Architecture.* Richmond: C.J. Hatcher. (Many references to lost inns and pubs).

Housman, J. 1814. *Descriptive Tour and Guide to the Lakes, Caves and Mountains and other Natural Curiosities in Cumberland, Westmorland, Lancashire and a Part of The West Riding of Yorkshire.* Carlisle: F. Jollie.

Howson, W. 1850. *An Illustrated Guide to the Curiosities of Craven.* London: Whittaker & Co; Settle: Wildman.

Hurtley, T. 1786. *A Concise Account of some Natural Curiosities in the Environs of Malham, in Craven, Yorkshire.* London: J. Robson and T. Longman.

Joynes, N.E. 2006. *The History of Carlton in Coverdale 1086 - 1910.* Unpublished PhD thesis, University of Leeds.

Lancaster, K.J. 1986. 'History of the White Hart'. *Sedbergh Historian* 2 (5).

Langcliffe Millennium Group. 2000. Langcliffe. *Glimpses of a Dales Village.* Settle: Hudson History.

Mass-Observation. 1987. *The Pub and the People.* Worktown Study. London: The Cresset Library.

Monckton, H.A. 1969. *A History of the English Public House.* London: The Bodley Head.

Morris, R. 2013. *Time's Anvil. England, Archaeology and the Imagination.* London: Phoenix, pp. 283-95. (On drinking, games and the church in post-medieval England).

Parr Maskell, H. 1929. *The Taverns of Old England.* London: Philip Alan.

Richardson, A.E. 1952. *The Old Inns of England.* London: Batsford.

Rigby, J. 1656. *An Ingenious Poem, called the Drunkards Prospective, or the Burning-Glasse.* London. (He was Clerk of the Peace for the County of Lancaster).

Riley, F. n.d. *Gleanings from a Yorkshire Valley. The Attractive Charm of Chapel-le-Dale.* Lancaster: Guardian Printing Works.

Scobie, J. 2010. 'On a glass of good ale: a history of ale and beer in Sedbergh' *Sedbergh Historian.* 6 (1), pp. 20-28.

Speight, H. 1897. *Romantic Richmondshire.* London: Elliot Stock.

Waters, C. 2005. *A Dictionary of Pub, Inn and Tavern Signs.* Newbury: Countryside Books.

Index of Featured Sites